ART OR NATURE

20th Century French Photography

IMAGES DE

FRANCE

Art or Nature: Twentieth Century French Photography has been organised as part of the programme of cultural exchanges between France and Great Britain, by the Association Française d'Action Artistique, under the auspices of the Ministre des Affaires Etrangères and the Ministre de la Culture et de la Communication of the French Republic.

This exhibition has been created with the help of the Bibliothèque Nationale (Cabinet des estampes et de la photographie), the Musée National d'Art Moderne, Centre Georges Pompidou, and the Centre National des Arts Plastiques, and with the generous support of Eurotunnel.

ART OR NATURE

20th Century French Photography

Agnès de Gouvion Saint-Cyr, Jean-Claude Lemagny, and Alain Sayag

Trefoil Publications Ltd, London
In association with Barbican Art Gallery

HONORARY COMMITEE

Honorary committee   **M. Jean-Bernard Raimond**
Ministre des Affaires Etrangères

M. François Léotard
Ministre de la Culture et de la Communication

Son Exc. M. Luc de la Barre de Nanteuil
Ambassadeur de France en Grande Bretagne

Co-ordinating Committee   **M. Louis Joxe**
Ambassadeur de France. Président de l'Association Française d'Action Artistique

M. Jean-Pierre Angremy
Directeur Général des Relations Culturelles, Scientifiques et Techniques au Ministère des Affaires Etrangères

M. Michel Boyon
Directeur du Cabinet du Ministre de la Culture et la Communication

M. Jean Maheu
Président du Centre Georges Pompidou

M. André Zavriew
Sous-directeur des Echanges Artistiques et Culturels au Ministère des Affaires Etrangères.
Directeur de l'Association Française d'Action Artistique

M. Philippe Guillemain
Conseiller Culturel près l'Ambassade de France en Grande Bretague

M. Jean-Claude Moyret
Sécretaire Général de l'Association Française d'Action Artistique

M. Pascal Bonafoux
Responsable du Bureau des Arts Plastiques à l'Association Française d'Action Artistique

Exhibition Organisers   **Agnès de Gouvion Saint-Cyr**
Chargée de mission pour la photographie au Ministère de la Culture et
de la Communication

Jean-Claude Lemagny
Conservateur au Cabinet des estampes de la Bibliothèque Nationale

Alain Sayag
Conservateur au Musée National d'Art Moderne, Centre Georges Pompidou

Corinne Henry
Association Française d'Action Artistique
Ministère des Affaires Etrangères, Bureau des Arts Plastiques

Brigitte Lardinois
Barbican Art Gallery

MESSAGE FROM THE CO-CHAIRMEN, EUROTUNNEL

We are delighted to be lead sponsor of 'Images de France'.

It seemed especially appropriate that the first Franco-British company, privately funded from both sides of the Channel, should support an exhibition where a few of the glories of French culture and civilisation can be appreciated in Great Britain. The opportunity for Londoners and visitors to see and participate in such a wide variety of events and exhibitions will draw our two countries closer together.

Something similar, on a larger scale, will follow from our own enterprise as it progresses. It will draw us closer and reinforce our common ties and purposes. Both of our countries are part of an integrated Europe while remaining heterogeneous and rich in our respective cultures.

Eurotunnel sets an example. It is an industrious and entrepreneurial organisation, whose French and British employees pursue corporate objectives in a spirit of co-operation and enthusiasm, bringing to their task the strengths of both systems.

We are pioneers in this type of organisation, as we are in the transport system we are developing. Where we go, others will follow. 'Images de France' is a celebration of some of the riches we can enjoy together.

André Bénard   Co-chairmen, Eurotunnel.   Alastair Morton

EURO TUNNEL ™

AUTHORS' ACKNOWLEDGEMENTS

We would particularly like to thank the following:

Monsieur Emmanuel Leroy-Ladurie, Administrateur Général de la Bibliothèque Nationale; Madame Laure Baumont, conservateur du Cabinet des Estampes de la Bibliothèque Nationale;
Monsieur Jean Maheu, Président du Centre Georges Pompidou; Monsieur Jean-Hubert Martin, Directeur du Musée National d'Art Moderne;
Monsieur Dominique Bozo, Délégué aux Arts Plastiques;

Madame Brassaï, M. et Mme Bihl-Bellmer, le Centre National d'Etudes Spatiales, Madame Michèle Chomette, Madame de Fenoÿl, Monsieur Paviot, Monsieur Petit, the Royal Photographic Society, Monsieur Treillard, Madame Izis;

The Rapho and Magnum agencies, and all the artists who have agreed to take part in this exhibition and publication.

In the catalogue, measurements are given in centimetres, height preceding width. The following lenders are identified in abbreviation: M.N.A.M. Musée National d'Art Moderne, Centre Georges Pompidou, B.N. Bibliothèque Nationale, F.N.A.C. Fonds National d'Art Contemporain.

CONTENTS

IMAGES DE FRANCE

This festival and *Art or Nature* in particular, illustrates how France in the first half of the twentieth century was the forcing ground for intellectual and artistic ideas with Paris as the central attraction for both native and foreign talents. The majority of photographers in this exhibition are French-born but included among them is an important selection from as wide a variety of foreign places as Hungary, Lithuania, Germany, Austria, Belgium, America and Japan. The presence of these foreign artists in Paris was as important to the development of photography in France as was the influence of French culture in turn upon the culture of their own countries.

As with a number of other exhibitions at the Barbican Art Gallery, *Art or Nature* seeks to show an area of work that has been over-looked or under assessed. While there have been exhibitions in this country of some of the major figures in this exhibition, there has never been a major study of French twentieth century photography, nor even a major book on the subject published here, so this area of activity seemed a perfect choice as the visual art centre-piece for the festival *Images de France* at the Barbican Centre.

French visual culture in the twentieth century has been dominated by painting and the exponents of photography have had to campaign hard to assert their work as a legitimate art form during this period. *Art or Nature* reveals how the Pictorialists, represented here by Demachy and Puyo, matched the leaders of the Paris Salon in their pursuit of aesthetic ideals and in so doing created an eroticism that was more immediately blatant than that of the heirs of Ingres. By comparison Atget, as much a chronicler of the demi-monde, died in obscurity, only to be rediscovered by a younger generation, more sensitive to the sinister isolation that Atget's unpeopled environment communicates.

The inter-war generations of photographers, too, competed in an arena dominated by the major painterly and literary figures and it was not until the fifties that *rapportage* photography came first to be recognised as standing independently. Since then the diversity of approaches to art practice with so many cross-media influences have allowed photographers and painters alike to sail close to each others' shorelines, leaving the position of photography duly established and respected in its own right.

In the period covered by this exhibition, while photographers have had to fight to be recognised as artists in their own right, their medium has had an untold influence upon the painters and film-makers of the century. The work of Atget, so lonely in its unpeopled isolation, struck a perfect chord for the Surrealists engrossed in their studies of psychological privation. The technical innovations that Man Ray and others introduced, opened up a welter of manipulative possibilities for artists and film-makers alike to exploit, and the instant and intimate observations of Brassaï showed how a rapid or automatic response to visual stimuli could create as telling an image as the more studied compositions of painters.

The selection of exhibits has been made in order to show how the two currents of 'Art' and 'Nature' have been pursued or allowed to intermingle in the photography of the period. While photography has come to stand on its own beside other visual art forms, the exponents of the medium too have had to grapple with the technical and intellectual possibilities that the medium offers. This exhibition clearly illustrates how a photograph can be as considered in its composition, impressive in its aesthetic quality as the most painstaking and beautiful art of a painter. Equally we can see how the natural reality in a photograph, capturing in a transitory moment an image of devastating visual impact, questions how the purely documentary can be divorced from the artistic in the work of a brilliant photographer like Kertész or Cartier-Bresson.

Barbican Art Gallery is indebted to l'Association Française d'Action Artistique, Ministère des Affaires Etrangères for its guidance and help in the preparation of this exhibition. This is the second instance of the gallery receiving such considerable support from this quarter, following the opening of the *Aftermath* exhibition in March 1982. The gallery is also particularly grateful for the generous sponsorship provided by Eurotunnel, the sponsors of the *Images de France* festival.

Finally this exhibition is the result of diligent work by the three selectors, Agnès de Gouvion Saint-Cyr, of the Mission pour la Photographie, Jean-Claude Lemagny of the Bibliothèque Nationale and Alain Sayag of Musée National d'Art Moderne, Centre Pompidou. They have chosen images, pursued contributors and negotiated loans in such a way as to make *Art or Nature* a memorable event.

John Hoole
Curator Barbican Art Gallery

Eugène Atget *Kiosque à journaux, Square du Bon Marché,* Newspaper kiosk, Paris 1912 (55)

INTRODUCTION

'The camera is a sketch book, an instrument of intuition and spontaneity, the master of the instant which, in visual terms, questions and decides simultaneously. In order to give a meaning to the world, one has to feel oneself involved in what one frames through the viewfinder.'* This vision of photography, which we owe to Henri Cartier-Bresson, sees photography as both natural and spontaneous. It is a view that has been accepted in France for almost fifty years. It has brought glory and fame to what is called 'humanistic reportage'; to personalities as diverse as Izis, Doisneau, or Boubat who have become well known. But while this method of working insists on the moral involvement of the photographer in his subject, it also seeks to be aesthetically neutral. In this way the humanistic reportage approach conforms to a 'common sense' view that subjects 'the photographic choice to the categories and the rules of traditional vision'. In so doing it treats photography as the 'natural' vehicle of objective realistic representation.

Nevertheless, as was the case nearly one hundred years ago, today a kind of photography has appeared that expresses an imaginary universe, that not only seems remote or even outside time, but, what is more, quite incompatible with the notion of photographic clarity and objectivity. The very precision of the descriptive system no longer occupies all the space available, making it not impossible but possible for any space for dreams or the imaginative to compete.

Little by little, we have begun to move back to a clearer vision, and in so doing we have rediscovered the first truth, so well expressed by Egon Schiele from the depths of his prison, that 'art is incapable of being modern'. Art is forever returning to its origins. Take for example the current pre-occupation with Post-Modernism. In one way it can be seen as a definitive juncture between art and fashion, leaving them merged in a sort of hedonism for the despairing. The other view, on the contrary, separates art from fashion for once and for all in order to restore a basic structure for truth and internal tension. Art, in effect, concerns truth; beauty is the sole and only sign. Furthermore, it is in the work that it resides, not in the manner of making the work. Art takes its existence from the irreconcilable aspect of works of art, from their inexplicable conflict, between them and with the world of men as it is.

What is to become of photography in all this? 'Progress is the paganism of imbeciles' said Baudelaire, and we can never shout this often enough. If Baudelaire condemned photography, it was because of its economic and social connections, and these have not ceased since to be a threat. Photography has for long allowed itself to be carried passively on the wings of fashionable theories: will it now come crashing to the ground? Or will it learn how to find that timeless element within itself, which the other arts have learnt through a process of exploration of their own material, of their very natures? For beauty can only result from an incarnation that is as complete as possible.

Agnès de Gouvion Saint-Cyr, Jean-Claude Lemagny and Alain Sayag

* Paul Hill and Thomas Cooper: Dialogue with Photography.
London: Thames and Hudson, 1979, p.76

Constant Puyo *Tête de Gorgone,* Gorgon's head, between 1894 and 1902. (30)

PICTORIALISM

In 1914, at the very height of his fame, Robert Demachy, the leader of the French Pictorialist movement, abruptly abandoned photography. He never gave his reasons for doing so, though he confirmed that his work was complete by allowing a retrospective exhibition, with his friend Constant Puyo, in 1931. The Pictorialist movement continued for a further ten years with a new generation of photographers such as Laure Albin-Guillot producing their best work in that time. But Demachy's decision signalled the beginning of the decline of the movement. Such abrupt decisions were nothing new. Twenty years before, Henry Peter Emerson, often considered one of the founders of the Pictorialist movement, proclaimed 'the death of the naturalistic photography'. After ten years searching for 'sentiment and poetry' he suddenly saw it as a technique that was incapable of giving any artistic satisfaction. Although Demachy would probably not have said exactly this, he did denounce in some of his writings 'this mechanical system which we have so persistently fought. The photographic character is, and always has been, an anti-artistic character, and the mechanically produced print from an untouched negative will always have, in the eyes of the true artist, faults in values and absences of accents against which the special qualities so loudly proclaimed will not count for much'.[1] 'The pure photographer can choose his subject: that is all. And with many apologies to the majority of photographers who think otherwise, it is very little; it is not enough. After this he is the slave of a stupid machine that lies and blunders even in the literal record of his motive.'[2] However Demachy went on to say that Pictorialism might finally allow photography to aspire to art.

Whether photography could so aspire was avidly discussed by the many groups of photography enthusiasts forming in Europe and America in opposition to the old photography associations. The Vienna Camera Club, established in 1891, aimed to promote a more elitist conception of photography than that of the Imperial Photographic Society. Their exhibitions accepted only photographs that were 'works of art'. Three years later the Photo Club de Paris was founded and held exhibitions in the luxurious salons of the Cercle Artistique et Littéraire at the Rue de Volney. They accepted works that 'in addition to technical excellence, presented a real artistic interest.'

The desire to raise this 'mechanical art' to fine art was primarily a reaction to the multiplication of images increasingly made possible by the simplification of production methods. From the 1880's technical achievements, such as easy to handle cameras (like the first Kodaks) and films on rolls and for development by the producer, made photography available to all. The public was now no longer buying photographs (making it harder to make a living as a photographer) but instead buying the means of taking them, and employing these means to take social rather than 'artistic' photographs. Faced with a proliferation of images which were judged to be of little merit, since there was no aesthetic control of them, a number of enlightened and affluent members of the bourgeoisie reacted; 'since science had put photography within everyone's reach, it was now necessary to place the mechanical image under the aegis of a master susceptible to guarantee the privileges of a few, a master situated at the opposite extreme of science, bearing a magical and prestigious name: *art*'[3].

This attitude was echoed by the desire of the best artists and critics of the times to 'escape from that shame of modern taste, from that base advertisement; those pavements swarming with a hideous crowd in search of money, of women degraded by childbirth and dulled by loathful commerce, of men reading infamous newspapers or dreaming of fornication and swindle all along the shops from which bandits established in commerce and banks spy upon them in order to rob them.'[4]

Photographers took pleasure in the reality of vulgarity whereas painters aspired to beautiful ideas. But photographers too could not escape from that quest for the ideal and the Pictorialists multiplying the veils of twilight, shadows and reflection were able to use them to escape from merely reproducing reality. This was not done, as suggested by the proponents of 'photographic clarity', to simply 'reproduce the effects already produced by painting,'[5] but to bring photography to the level of painting. One of the aims of Pictorialists whether they wrote about it like Robert de la Sizeranne[6] or practised it, like Demachy and Puyo, was to make photography a means of expression with its own place in the fine arts. As academics they did not accept that a mechanical copy of nature could be a work of art; 'The photographer is absolutely powerless, because he uses a machine, to emphasise and to suppress. And the essence of Art consists in emphasis and suppression.'[7]

The many technical processes, which were then being used — Demachy mentions nine; platinotype, carbon, gum bichromate, gum ozotype, ozotype, Fresson, Artigue, Hochmeister and oils[8] — were destined not to create "an increasing resemblance between photography and oil paintings, drawing, etching and lithography"[9] in order to to satisfy an uncultivated public. It is not a matter of "a superficial and ideologically false" process to go against that which is justly characteristic of photographic images: "its clarity". But of a transcendental conception of Beauty to which one can only attend by eliminating the trivial, superfluous and mediocre. For Demachy a good photograph needed more than correct composition and lighting; it needed 'true values, true tone, true rendering of texture and what we call in French studio language 'une belle matière' a pigment which will allow rich transparent shadows and delicate and fluid half-tones.'[10] He added 'I must be a little mad in that area, for a beautiful smudge of Indian Ink on white, creamy paper will interest me much more than many an elaborate bromide picture.'[11]

Photography sought not to imitate painting but to be inspired by it and so to create classic works that transcended eras and styles. In such a situation it mattered little about the performance of the material and canonical rules of the shot as their role no longer took precedence over the realisation of the thing that flowered from them, the 'innate gift' that no teaching, no manual no matter how detailed is capable of instilling. Following this Demachy and Puyo warned photographers that in using the gum bichromate process they should, according to consecrated expression, be self-taught. 'A treatise could no more teach the secret of a perfect gum than grammar teaches the art of writing.'[12]

The Pictorialist movement with its homogeneous social composition and its tight aesthetic theory kept a relatively unified output beyond the First World War despite its international nature. Yet even as it reached its peak between 1905 and 1910 it bore within it the ferment of its decline. The Beaux-Arts system from which it derived had been in crisis for the past thirty years. The Salon was no longer what it had been in the middle of the nineteenth century. It was under attack both from inside, by artists such as Ernest Meissonier and Pierre Puvis de Chavannes who contested the right of the Institute de France to rule artistic life entirely, and from outside by the artistic world who called for Salons without jury and prizes. More serious still was the rise of new aesthetic ideas which would radically question the search for technical 'excellence' on which Pictorialism was based. But it was the war that, ending an era of peace and relative social consensus in Europe, would condemn the values of the Pictorialists. The dusky tones and pictorialist half-light, that 'stifling atmosphere' of the turn-of-the-century, would brutally be cast away by images that removed the 'make-up from reality'[13] and exposed the cruel truth of man's relations with the world.

Alain Sayag
Conservateur au Musée National d'Art Moderne, Centre Georges Pompidou

1. Reprint in Bill JAY: Robert Demachy, photographs and essays, Academy Ltd, London, 1974, p.29

2. Robert DEMACHY: Mechanism and Pictorial Photography, The Amateur Photographer, 11 June 1907, reprint in Bill JAY, p.31

3. Marc MELON: Au-delà du réel, la photographie d'art, in Histoire de la photographie, under the direction of J. C. LEMAGNY and A. ROUILLE, éditions Bordas, Paris, 1986, p.85

4. J. K. HUYSMANS: L'Art moderne, collection 10/18, Paris, 1975, p.258

5. Jean-Luc DAVAL: histoire d'un Art, la Photographie, éditions Skira, Genève, 1982. p.117

6. Robert de Sizeranne's 'La photographie est-elle un Art?' in La Revue des Deux Mondes, 1898 is always cited; however one might also evoke all Pictorialist authors, who were forever raising this question.

7. R. DEMACHY, reprint in Bill JAY, 1974

8. R. DEMACHY: on exhibition catalogues, The Amateur Photographer, 11 June 1907, reprint in Bill JAY, 1974, p.31

9. Giséle FREUND; Photographie et Société, éditions du Seuil, Paris, 1974, p.89

10. R. DEMACHY: What difference is there between a good photograph and an artistic photograph, Camera Notes, 2 October 1899, reprint in Bill JAY, 1974, p.23

11. R. DEMACHY: The Gum print, Camera Work, July 1904, reprint in Bill JAY. 1974, p.27

12. Marc MELON in Histoire de la photographie, 1986, p.86

13. Walter BENJAMIN: Petite histoire de la photographie, in L'homme, le langage et la culture, éditions Denoël, Paris, 1971

Constant Puyo *Sans titre (devant la cheminée),* Untitled (by the fire), 1899. (27)

Robert Demachy *Désespoir,* Despair, n.d. (14)

Robert Demachy *Perplexité,* Perplexity, n.d. (5)

Robert Demachy *Souvenir no 2*, n.d. (12)

Robert Demachy *Timide,* The timid one, n.d. (6)

Constant Puyo *L'atelier du photographe,* The Photographer's studio, between 1894 and 1902. (28)

Constant Puyo *Untitled,* between 1894 and 1902. (19)

Eugène Atget *Boulanger,* Baker, 1898. (34)

RAPPORTAGE I

Shaken by the Franco-Prussian conflict, wounded by the drama of the Commune, French society at the turn of the century had become aware of the fragility of its structures and, while the external world crumbled, photography was expected to provide an objective testimony to social reality and aspects of life that preoccupied intellectuals and politicians alike.

At the same time, supporters of artistic photography became mobilised and their theories spread across the world, through articles and manifestoes, creating a very marked aesthetic current. It is not the least of photography's paradoxes that two diametrically opposed concepts, objectivism and Pictorialism, were developed at the dawn of the twentieth century.

Eugène Atget and Jacques-Henri Lartigue, both exceptional personalities, neither allied to particular camps, were to realign the notion of *rapportage* while at the same time linking it to a more aesthetic conception of photography. After having tried various métiers, Atget began as a photographer of landscape, intended as backgrounds for painters. It was not until 1897 that he decided to undertake a disciplined and methodical project of photographing all that 'is artistic and picturesque in Paris and its surroundings'. A tireless walker, loaded with his heavy equipment - camera, tripod and glass plates - Atget scoured the streets of Paris in search of architectural elements threatened by time or human thoughtlessness.

Thought to be naive, Atget was rigorous to the point of obsession; his photographs were documents but his lyrical mission was the opposite of a cold sociological report. In this way his work marked the culminating point of one tradition while also reforming itself into another. Given an architectural work, Atget explored it and recreated it within its own space, emphasised by the use of wide angles and the almost total absence of figures that might disturb the timeless quality of the image. Once the spaces and volumes had been demarcated he became interested in the details - statues, sign boards, staircases or doorknobs - nothing seemed insignificant to him. With an impressive lucidity Atget freed the object from its natural environment, often leaving to the sun the task of burning out unwanted or intrusive elements.

This 'photographer-archaeologist', as Atget liked to call himself, was also much attracted to the daily life of ordinary people and, when the illustrator André Dignimont commissioned a work about prostitutes he had in mind the humane and caring *rapportage* that Atget had already done on craftsmen, beggars, gypsies and concierges.

Through an unexpected combination of circumstances, Atget, who had never underestimated the artistic dimensions of his photographs, became a hero to the avant-garde of his time. In effect, Man Ray, one of his frequent clients, introduced him to the Surrealists who published some of his works. They, along with the Cubists, were the first to detect the poetic and artistic force of Atget's oeuvre and when, after the artist's death, Pierre MacOrlan published *Atget photographe de Paris* in 1930, the photographer's fame was to extend well beyond France.

The gaze that Jacques-Henri Lartigue cast over his contemporaries was the result of a very different method - that of the enlightened amateur filling the pages of a family journal. Born into a wealthy family that numbered many artists and inventors, the young boy discovered that by opening and closing his eyes rapidly he succeeded in capturing images that were ephemeral and yet stamped with real materials, colours and sounds. His father gave him a camera, his 'eye-trap' with which he created his family album: parents and friends, their fantasies, their inventions, their elegance or their extravagance. He took a very simple, almost physical pleasure in seeing time arrested on an image, so that his 'memory, a sort of hunter installed in his brain, preserved things of the past'.

Although he had lived through two major wars, Lartigue only wanted to retain life's happy moments: women's beauty, the elegance of their fashions, the speed of automobiles and the drama of flight. He did not ignore pain and unhappiness but felt it was useless to become weighed down by them. But we should not be fooled by Lartigue's role of nonchalance, he was capable of an extraordinary formal rigour and mastery in the treatment of light and an incomparable boldness in the use of décadrage and 'stopping on the image'. Being a painter, Lartigue photographed principally for his own pleasure, only accepting commissions (from *Life, Paris Match* or *Vogue* for example) under exceptional circumstances and thus remained faithful to the line taken by amateur photographers since the nineteenth century. Strange destiny for work which, almost at the same time, was presented at the Museum of Modern Art in New York (1963) and published in a book entitled *Les photographies de Jacques-Henri Lartigue*, a family album of the Belle Epoque (1966).

If the First World War somewhat eclipsed the technical discoveries favouring photography's growth, in particular the invention of the gelatin-bromide print, the mechanisation of reproduction and the amelioration of the transmission of images, nonetheless the years between the wars. with their intermixing of cultures, the circulation of new ideas and flowering of publications, remain a period of unequalled creativity in the domain of *rapportage*.

Still stunned by the last echoes of the war, Europeans were avid for truth - they wanted to see and understand. With the appearance of the Leica camera and 35mm film, photographers were now able to tell a story by the use of a sequence of organised images in an intentional way. Photographers who now had the power to see and to show, searched for more effect: aware of avant-garde movements, they allowed themselves much boldness: high and low angle shots, unusual lighting, manipulations or transformations of forms. At the same time, editors of reviews and magazines went beyond a journalistic role and became themselves designers.

Without Stefan Lorant in Germany and England, Lucien Vogel in France or Henry Luce in the USA, talents like Kertèsz, Brassaï, Brandt or Cartier-Bresson would not have been able to express themselves with such freedom.

Employed in a bank in Budapest, though much interested in photography, André Kertész had served as a soldier in the Hungarian army and kept a photographic diary of the war. Fascinated by Paris he decided to move there in 1926 and soon, involved in the avant-garde movements, received his first commissions. He began as a portraitist, then changed to *rapportage*, with commissions for German magazines and then for the *Revue des Médecins* and *Art et Médecine*, before working regularly for Lucien Vogel and *Vu*. There he imposed his way of seeing, with its unsettled perspective, developing the idea that 'the purest photography might hide a distortion and a subjective stand'. Kertèsz's taste for the unusual brought him close to Surrealism, but he remained a reporter attentive to the world and its minutiae, a photographer who experimented with everything - deformations of bodies underwater, distortions of nudes in a mirror, even aerial perspectives..

Hungarian also, Brassaï arrived in Paris at around the same time as Kertèsz, after his studies at the School of Fine Arts in Budapest. He frequented the same artists as his compatriot, but having a wider range of talents, he began by writing, painting and drawing. His first photographs appeared in *Le Minotaure* followed by his graffiti and his versions of Picasso's sculptures. He moved away from abstraction for a while in order to devote his energies in quest of the strange and disconcerting world of the night. The publication of his book *Paris de Nuit* in 1933 was a great success and from then he took photographs for *Verve* or *Harper's Bazaar* of people, their customs and environment with that lucid vision that made him interested in the prosaic, the ridiculous or even the absurd and vulgar. This preoccupation linked him to a line of photographers from Weegee to William Klein, without forgetting Lisette Model or Diane Arbus, who posed a critical, not to say, grating eye on society.

Was the success of these publications due to the public's affirmed taste for photography or did the demands of readers lead to the creation of books and magazines of such quality? The very fine photoengraving and the almost general use of gravure printing, which confers a palpable density on the images, confirm that photography was never treated so well. In this respect Emmanuel Sougez left his mark through his role as director of photographic services for *Illustration* and as consultant to Charles Peignot.

Charles Peignot was an audacious man who, fascinated by typography and the graphic, took on publication of the review *Arts et Métiers Graphiques* in 1930. After somewhat difficult beginnings, Peignot decided to publish a special issue on photography in order to save the magazine. The immediate success of this initiative led him to dedicate one issue each year, up until the war, to photography. Bill Brandt, Brassaï, Nora Dumas, Germaine Krull, André Kertèsz, Emmanuel Sougez and René Zuber found favourable ground for their works. Henri Cartier-Bresson published his first photograph in this magazine.

Lucien Vogel, more politically involved than Peignot, founded the weekly magazine *Vu* in 1928 followed by *Regards* and *Vu et Lu*. His contributors included the most prestigious photographers - Munkasci, Capa, Kertèsz and Krull -and famous writers like Phillipe Soupault. Vogel expressed his aim in the magazine's first issue, and special issues were devoted to the most difficult subjects, such as, '*Vu* in Soviet Countries', 'The German Enigma' or 'Year XI of Fascism'.

In the United States, Henry Luce followed the same principle when he founded the magazine *Life* in 1936, which would take over from *Vu* when it folded in 1938. Certain magazines were marked by a collaboration with one photographer, for example, Robert Doisneau and his association with *Le Point*, while others were created by means of an 'industrial patronage' that produced them for their clients and allowed photographers freedom of expression. *Art et Médecine*, is an exemplary magazine, which, as was the custom of the time, linked the creativity of writers and photographers. An identical phenomenon occurred in the editorial domain when the publisher Gallimard paved the way magnificently with the publication of *Voyage au Congo*, (1929) by André Gide, with photographs by the young Marc Allégret.

The rise of Nazism in Europe ended this impressive creativity; numerous photographers, often of Jewish origin, were forced to flee at the height of their careers. Some left their homes for the USA, such as Kertèsz: others, like Brassaï abandoned *rapportage* for more personal work, while others pursued their work more clandestinely, as did Doisneau and Cartier-Bresson or were witnesses from abroad like Gisèle Freund. The work of this 'second generation' of *rapportage* is the subject of a later section (p. 72). Here in the work of Atget and Lartigue we are among the last independent photographers, and in Kertèsz and Brassaï two of the first to work with the new magazines.

Agnès de Gouvion Saint-Cyr
Chargée de mission pour la photographie au Ministère de la Culture et de la Communication

Eugène Atget *Marchand de parapluies,* Umbrella vendor, 1898. (54)

Above: **Eugène Atget** *Roulotte, porte d'Italie,* Travelling cart, porte d'Italie, Paris, 1912. (42)

Facing page top: **Eugène Atget** *Moulin á Charenton,* Mill at Charenton, n.d. (40)

Facing page bottom: **Eugène Atget** *Hangar de l'auberge du Compas d'Or, rue Montorgueil,* Cart shed at the Compas d'Or inn, Paris, n.d. (48)

Eugène Atget *Au Bon Croix, rue des Haudriettes, Paris,* before 1908. (61)

Eugène Atget *Boutique, 16 rue Dupetit-Thouars, Paris,* 1912. (56)

Brassaï *Paris de nuit,* Paris by night, 1932. (77) © Mme G. Brassaï

Brassaï *Couple d'amoureux dans un café,* Lovers in a café, 1932. (72) © Mme G. Brassaï

Brassaï *Paris de nuit: Chez Suzy,* Paris by night: Chez Suzy about 1932. (78). © Mme G. Brassaï

Brassaï *Un Complet pour deux, bal Magic City,* Young couple sharing the same suit, about 1931. (82) © Mme G. Brassaï

Top: **Jacques-Henri Lartigue** *Bibi, London, October,* 1926. (97)

Above: **Jacques-Henri Lartigue** *Au Carlton, Vichy, août 1922,* At the Carlton, Vichy, August 1922. (91)

Facing page: **Jacques-Henri Lartigue** *Chouchou, tournage de 'Feu' de Baroncelli,* Chouchou shooting 'Fire' by Baroncelli, Epinay, December 1926. (96)

Jacques-Henri Lartigue *Mamie, Bibi et Jean le chauffeur,* Mamie, Bibi and Jean the chauffeur: Hispano-Suiza 32 HP car on the road to Houlgate, April 1927. (106)

Jacques-Henri Lartigue *Gerard Willemetz and Dani, Royan, July,* 1926. (95)

Jacques-Henri Lartigue *Bibi, l'ombre et le reflet,* Bibi, Shadow and Reflection, Hendaye, August 1927. (102)

André Kertèsz *Dubo, Dubon, Dubonnet,* 1934. (135)

André Kertèsz *Une fenêtre, quai Voltaire,* A window in the quai Voltaire, Paris, 1928. (121)

André Kertèsz *Danseur burlesque,* Burlesque dancer, 1926. (119)

André Kertèsz *Distortion no. 40,* 1933. (134)

André Kertèsz *Martinique,* 1972. (141)

André Kertèsz *Trottoir,* Pavement, 1929. (115)

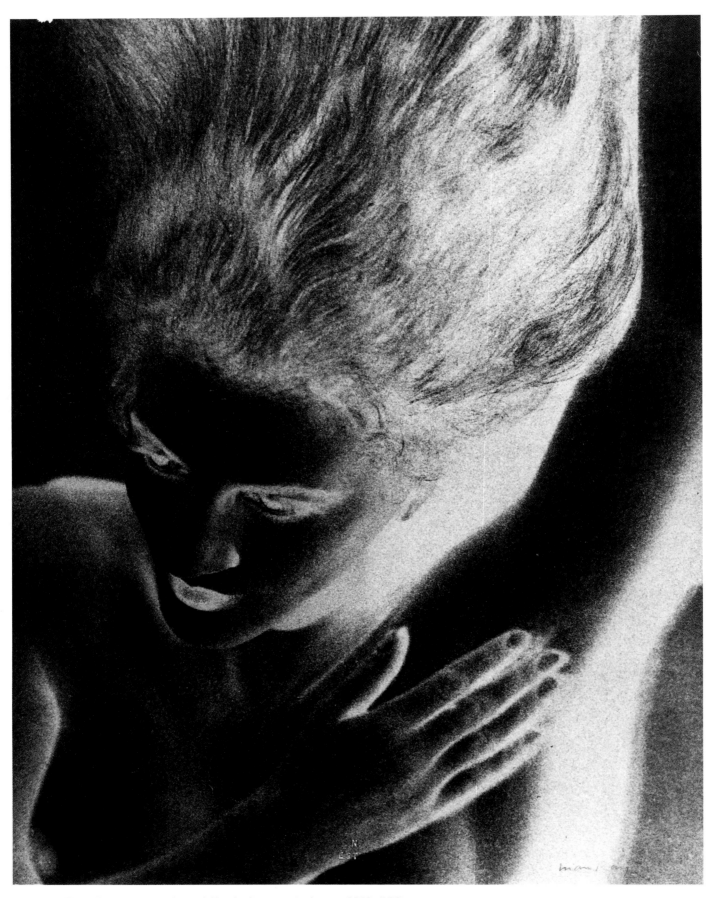

Man Ray *Tête (d'après un autochrome),* Head, after an autochrome, 1929. (176)

DADA AND SURREALISM

Violent changes or innovations have, more often than not, been taken as the marking points in the history of the twentieth century. When it comes to establishing the history of photography, then either the emphasis is on the many technical and social innovations that set the tempo for its course of development, or photography is linked to the Fine Arts and the correlations with the great crises that divide 'modern' art are what is noted.

Within such a view of history, Surrealism appears as one of the greatest rifts of the twentieth century - one of the succession of fundamental 'isms' whose evolution has led to the modernity that is ours today. Within this iconoclastic 'negation of tradition, becoming a search for the new, singular and surprising, that has in turn been elevated to the status of tradition'[1] Man Ray has a special place. In his memoirs, published in 1963, he insisted at great length on the freedom that this 'game' or research meant for him. 'Art is neither a science nor an experiment. There is no more progress in art than in flirting. I'm simply trying to be as free as possible in my way of working and in the choice of my subject matter. No one gives me orders or guides me. One might criticise me afterwards, but then it's too late. The work has been done. I have tasted freedom.'[2]

In 1921, he by chance discovered 'a process for taking photographs without a camera' which he called Rayographs; 'a sheet of photo paper got into the developing tray - a sheet unexposed that had been mixed with those already exposed under the negatives... and as I waited in vain a couple of minutes for an image to appear regretting the waste of paper, I unthinkingly placed a small glass funnel, the graduate and the thermometer in the tray on the wetted paper. I turned on the light; before my eyes an image began to form, not quite a simple silhouette of the objects as in a straight photograph, but distorted and refract by the glass more or less in contact with the paper. I made a few prints taking whatever objects came to hand; my hotel-room key, a handkerchief, some pencils, a brush, a candle, a piece of twine - it wasn't necessary to put them in the liquid for a few seconds as with negatives...'[3] Another example of these accidental discoveries is solarization. Lee Miller, at one time Man Ray's assistant, tells how once while developing photographs she stumbled and accidentally turned on the light, causing a halo of light to be formed around the image which was in the process of being developed.[4].

And therefore from both the technical standpoint - rayographs were not so new after all - and the aesthetic level, Man Ray stands within a tradition. Of this he was perfectly aware, so that we find that when he writes about the manner in which solarisation accentuates the lines of a composition there are references to the most 'classical' painters - Botticelli or Ingres. Is there not here a considerable degree of confusion. On the one hand the author often insists on the radical quality of his practice while on the other he makes abundant aesthetic references and 'his constant attraction to classicism'[5] is evident even to those who only look at the works.

Considering Surrealist photography in its entirety, the same stylistic disorders can be found. The range of choices adopted by the photographers is immense. For example there are images of a dismal banality such as those by Boiffard commissioned by André Breton as illustrations for *Nadja*. Or there are images that are close to the Nouvelle Objectivité such as those of Florence Henri or Dora Maar, or the series of Picasso's 'sculptures' taken by Brassaï. There are also more elaborate photographs resulting from manipulations of the camera or in the darkroom, to create that irrational, dream-like space that is generally associated with Surrealism. In this respect, a comparison might be made between Man Ray's solarisations and the work of Raoul Ubac. The techniques in both are certainly close, although Ubac invented new finishes, such as burning or petrification (a printing process that gives the image the thickness of a bas relief and which Breton considered as 'one of the most fertile.')

However, Man Ray's elegant and delicate compositions - 'almost without relief, like drawings'[6], cannot be compared to the dramatic tension of Ubac's works. And the same comparison might be made between the technique of double exposure as used by Roger Parry or Maurice Tabard. Although Roger Parry studied at the Ecole des Beaux-Arts and the Ecole des Arts Décoratifs he was above all a professional photographer. His *Banalités*, published in 1930, is one of the most perfect illustrated Surrealist books. In order to illustrate Léon-Paul Fargue's text, Parry skilfully combined all the Surrealist tricks to obtain a series of images where the technical mastery and formal perfection are not take seriously but which always retain the spirit of an inventive and fruitful game.

This was not the case for Tabard, who was nevertheless one of the most appreciated and reproduced artists of the avant-garde in the 1930's. Even though he really only took part in the Surrealist movement for a very brief period from 1929-1931, he exploited all the possibilities of solarisation and superimposition in a formalism increasingly hollow and punctilious.

Indeed, the true singularity of Surrealist photography resides in its implication of travestied reality. 'Surrealist photography is in fact extremely artificial, even when it does not use double exposure, solarisation or other similar techniques.'[7] That this reconstruction of reality was evident, as in the case of Hans Bellmer's work, or whether it rests on a fundamental ambiguity as in the case of Brassaï, it nevertheless constitutes one of the most perfect successes of Surrealism.

Faced with the daily rise of intrusive and suspicious Nationalism in Berlin of 1933, Hans Bellmer decided to devote his energy to the construction 'slowly, limb by limb' of a life-sized doll. Photography, as a witness to the diverse metamorphoses of the construction, rapidly became the place where desire and dream were closely combined. The Doll 'suspected of being nothing but a representation and a fictitious reality' should go 'to find in the exterior world, in the shock of meetings, the certain proofs of its existence'[8]. Photography, through its immediacy and its facility to accommodate the slightest of the Doll's and the author's fantasies, becomes the privileged instrument of an intense and brutal creative activity. The Doll, moving about from the garden of the paternal property to the kitchen, sometimes broken and spread out on the floor, at other times hanging from a tree or a doorpost, appears in all the official publications and demonstrations of the Surrealist group. The Doll's presence is such that it might justifiably be considered as a perfect example of an artist's ability to take possession of the photographic medium in order to invest it with an aesthetic finality and thus satisfy an artistic ambition that is no less than 'the remedy and compensation for a certain impossibility to live'[9].

Although welcomed at the same time in Surrealist journals, the photographs of Brassaï were quite different. Everything in his works are very real, even prosaic. From the banks of the Saint-Martin canal to the brothels of the rue Saint-Denis, from the walls of the Santé prison to stairways in Montmartre, his is a universe drawn from the daily life. Indeed for Brassaï, it is the most sincere and humble appreciation of reality, the most everyday event that leads to the extraordinary. And thus it is no accident that when invited by Breton to join the Surrealist group, he always refused. He preferred to keep what Henry Miller called his 'normal vision', that 'faithfulness to the object'[10], that fear of betrayal, the 'obsessive pursuit for resemblance'[11] that compelled him, 'the creator of images to pour the living thing into the living form... To invent nothing, to imagine everything'[12].

Breton's avowed aversion for the real form of objects indicated the rejection of this form of realism that turns the privileged instant into a convincing proof of the universe that surrounds us. This rejection marks the continuity of a line of aesthetic research which makes the Surrealists our close contemporaries.

Alain Sayag
Conservateur au Musée National d'Art Moderne, Centre Georges Pompidou

1. Jean CLAIR: Considérations sur l'état des Beaux Arts, Paris, Gallimard, 1983, p.30

2. Some papers by MAN RAY, Copley Galleries, Beverly Hills, 1948, not paginated

3. MAN RAY: Self Portrait, Boston, Little Brown; London, André Deutsch, 1963, p128/129

4. But to set the record straight, a few years earlier in 1918 Christian Schad, one of the first Dadaists, had already applied this technique while in Zurich, and the work of one of the inventors of photography, W.H. Fox Talbot, recalls this process to some extent. In his *Self Portrait*, Man Ray remembers as a child having placed fern leaves on a blank frame and exposing them to sunlight just as Fox Talbot had done a century earlier.

5. Jane LIVINGSTON: MAN RAY and surrealist photography, in Rosalind KRAUSS and Jane LIVINGSTON: L'amour fou, New York, Abbeville Press, 1986

6. MAN RAY: op. cit., p.127

7. Rosalind KRAUSS: op. cit., p.91

8. Hans BELLMER: La poupée, Paris, G.L.M., 1936, not paginated

9. Unpublished letter from Hans BELLMER to Jean BRUN, dated April 3, 1946

10. BRASSAÏ: Contemporary Photographers, New York, MacMillan, 1922, p.101

11. Ibid.

12. BRASSAÏ, Paris, Ed. du Pont Neuf, 1952, notes, not paginated

Hans Bellmer *La poupée,* The doll, 1949. (155)

Roger Parry *Untitled,* about 1928-1930. (144)

Florence Henri *L'assiette et le miroir,* Saucer and mirror, 1931. (146)

Robert Bresson *Lunar landscape,* 1932. (150)

Brassaï *Graffiti: la mort,* Death, 1934. (158) © Mme G. Brassaï

Brassaï *Graffiti*, 1934. (156) © Mme G. Brassaï

Raoul Hausmann *La balançoire,* The swing, about 1948. (167)

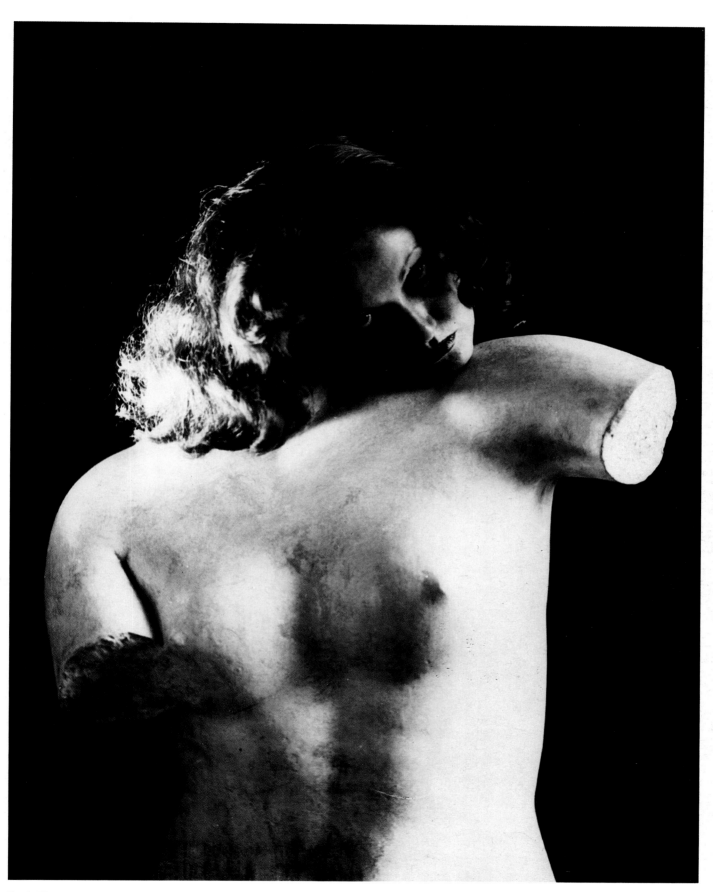

Erwin Blumenfeld *M's torso in mirror,* 1937/38. (171)

Jean Painlevé *Bust of a Sea-horse,* about 1930. (161)

Jacques-André Boiffard *Photogramme,* c. 1932/33. (164)

Man Ray *Objects,* 1926. (174)

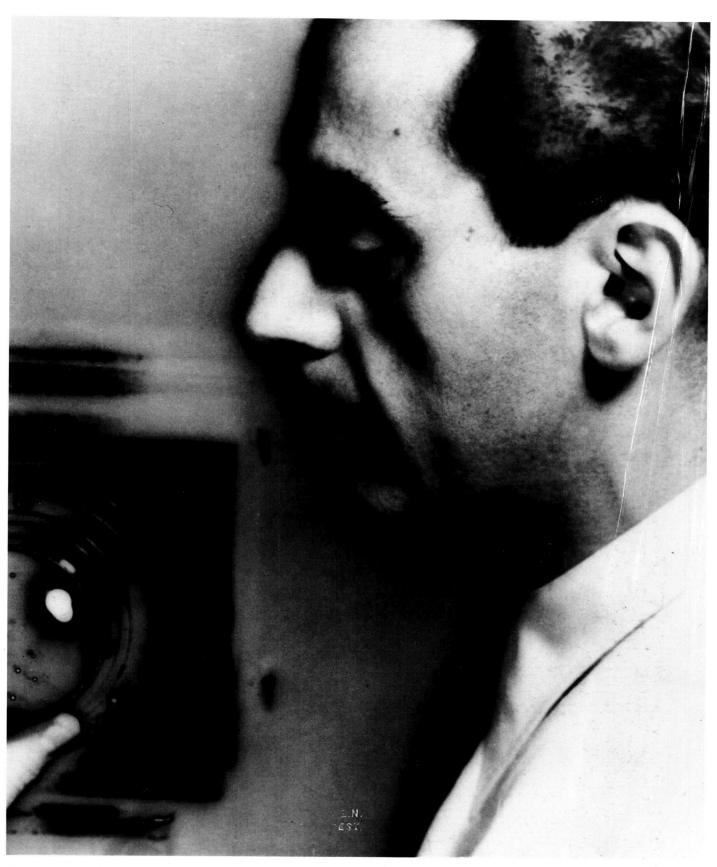

Man Ray *Autoportrait,* Self portrait, n.d. (189)

Man Ray *La Marquise Casati,* 1930. (180)

Man Ray *Femme endormie,* Sleeping woman, 1931. (181)

Man Ray *Noire et blanche,* Black and white, 1926. (198)

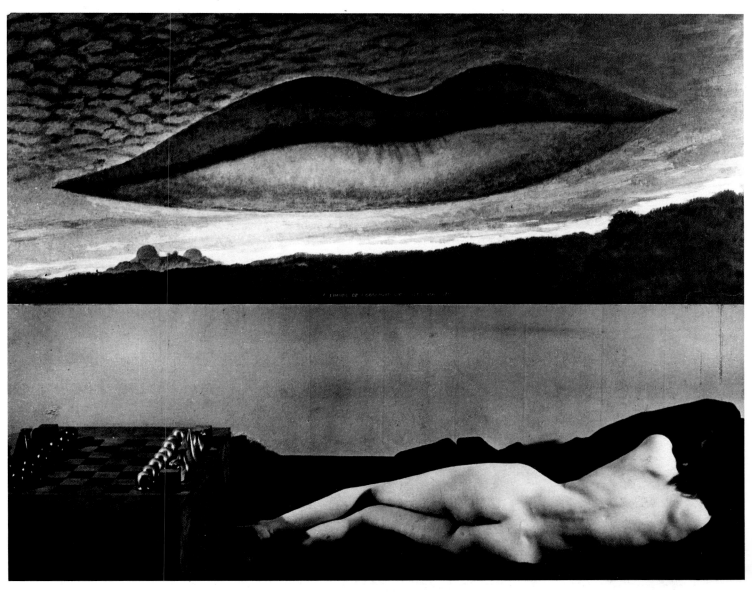

Man Ray *A l'heure de l'Observatoire, les amoureux, 1932,* At the hour of the Observatory, the lovers, 1932. (184)

Maurice Tabard *Tête au chapeau, oeil double,* Head with hat and double eye, 1929. (200)

Maurice Tabard *Untitled,* 1929. (201)

Raoul Ubac *Le combat de Penthésilée (14),* The combat of Penthesilea (14), 1937. (207)

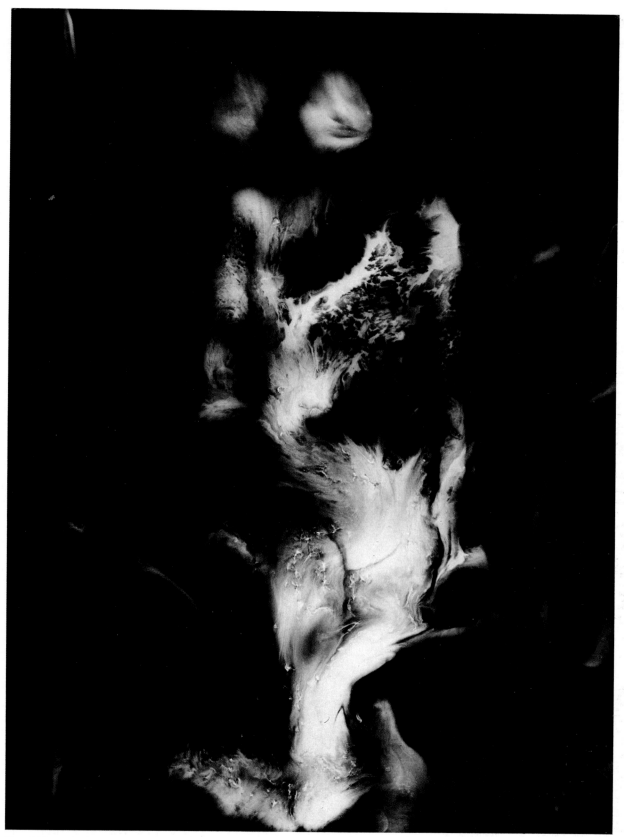

Raoul Ubac *La Nébuleuse,* Nebula, 1939. (211)

Robert Doisneau *Coco,* 1952. (254)

RAPPORTAGE II

Despite the shortages and poor quality of printing materials photographic *rapportage* was nonetheless to find a dynamism immediately after the war. Two explanations can doubtlessly be given for this revival: French society's anxiety after the horrors of the Second World War led to a thirst for images, and secondly, the period saw the development of photographic agencies that were in turn breeding grounds of talent. Following the Dephot agency in Berlin and Associated Press in the USA, the Alliance Photo, Keystone and Rapho agencies appeared in Paris. These agencies put enormous efforts into selecting and distributing their photographers' work, and were increasingly concerned with the use made of all these images. European agencies closed down during the war also found a new vitality.

Under the guiding hands of Cartier-Bresson, Chim and Capa, the Magnum agency was created in 1947. These photographers shared a common ideal, to control the exploitation of their work, which itself was the testimony of a lucid and critical look at society. These photographers felt concerned with misery, social and racial injustice, and with war. Their involvement was through their cameras. Although Cartier-Bresson denied it, he played a determinant role within the agency, underlining that for the reporter 'photography is, in the same instant, the simultaneous recognition of the signification of a fact and the rigorous organisation of visually perceived forms that express and signify that fact.' The public discovered the truth of that analysis in *Images à la sauvette* published in 1952, which combined a subtle intelligence and an extreme formal rigour, a quality Cartier-Bresson so admired in the work of Kertèsz.

The opening of a New York branch made Magnum an international agency and with Bishof, Buri, Riboud and many others the agency set the tone for the 1950's and 1960's. Another outstanding agency in that period is Rapho, which took on a more optimistic approach to what might be described as humanist *rapportage*. Each of its members contributed their own personal note - Doisneau's was humour, Izis's poetry, Sabine Weiss's lyricism, Boubat's tenderness or Ronis's incisive nostalgia.

There were however certain photographers who continued to work independently. For example François Kollar, who photographed France at work for the publisher Horizons de France; Jean-Pierre Sudre and Jean Dieuzaide also worked extensively for publishers. As to magazines, Jean-Philippe Charbonnier and Denis Brihat travelled around the world for *Réalités* and Izis worked with *Paris Match*.

In 1956 the 'Family of Man' exhibition opened in Paris and New York. Organised by Edward Steichen over a period of three years, the exhibition was created in 'a passionate spirit of devoted love and faith in man'. The 503 photographs by 273 photographers constituted a 'camera testament, a drama of the grand canyon of humanity, an epic woven of fun, mystery and holiness'. The exhibition had considerable repercussions, because much current photographic activity had taken humanity as its fundamental subject. It also inspired many careers in *rapportage* as well as encouraging the boom of photography books published in the 1950's. Enterprising publishers like Tériade, Arthaud, Arts et Métiers Graphiques, Horizons de France, Le Cercle d'Art and Delpire in France and La Guilde du Livre in Lausanne successfully linked writers and photographers. Prévert and Izis presented *Paris des Rêves* (1950), Elsa Triolet and Robert Doisneau collaborated on *Pour que Paris soit* (1956) and Claude Roy and Paul Strand published *France de Profil* (1952). Other books were devoted only to the work of individual photographers: Ronis's *Belleville-Ménilmontant* (1955), Cartier-Bresson's *Moscou* (1955), William Klein's *New York* (1956) or Jean-Loup Sieff's *Ballet* (1961).

In the 1950's *Life* and *Paris Match* became the conscience of the world, presenting the last echoes of the war, reconstruction and then decolonization. But they were not the sole, essential sources of information for long. With the development of television, the practice of *rapportage* evolved, towards work for immediate use by newspapers and more structured work destined for magazines. The importance given to information often takes precedence over the quality of photographic creativity. And yet agencies like Sygma, Gamma or Sipa can be credited with having learnt how to adapt to radically different demands, for colour, for the sensational, the exceptional or the specific. What is there, then, in common between Atget and the award winners from World Press Photo? The answer must be not very much, except a shared and unequivocal fascination for the human condition.

Agnès de Gouvion Saint-Cyr
Chargée de mission pour la photographie au Ministère de la Culture et de la Communication

Robert Doisneau *Mademoiselle Anita du Dancing de 'La boule rouge',* Anita, from the dancehall 'La boule rouge',
rue de Lappe, Paris, 1951. (252)

Henri Cartier-Bresson *Au bord de la Marne,* On the banks of the Marne, France 1938. (225)

Henri Cartier-Bresson *Trieste (Italy),* 1933. (221)

Above: **William Klein** *Quatre têtes au coin de Broadway et la 33eme rue,* Four heads, corner of Broadway and 33rd St., 1954. (261)

Facing page, top: **William Klein** *Terasse de café, Paris,* Café terrace, Paris, 1980. (265)

Facing page, bottom: **William Klein** *Coney Island l'hiver, New York,* Coney Island in winter, New York, 1955. (263)

Robert Doisneau *Les baigneurs de La Varenne,* Bathers at La Varenne, 1945 (248)

Robert Doisneau *Un regard oblique,* A look sideways: painting by Wagner in the window of the Galerie Romi, rue de Seine, Paris, 1948. (250)

Robert Doisneau *Café Noir et Blanc,* The black and white café, avenue du Général Galliéni, Joinville le Pont, 1948. (249)

Robert Doisneau *Les gosses de la place Hebert,* Kids from the place Hebert, Paris, 1957. (260)

Izis *Cracheur de feu,* Fire-eater, 1959. (270)

Izis *Boulevard de Clichy* n.d. (273)

Izis *Lagny, parade pour une femme crocodile,* Lagny, the crocodile lady sideshow, 1959 (269)

Edouard Boubat *Petits garçons jouant à la guerre,* Parisian children playing at soldiers, 1954. (277)

Edouard Boubat *Enfants jouant dans la neige au jardin du Luxembourg,* Children playing in the snow, Luxembourg gardens, Paris, 1955. (278)

Edouard Boubat *A la manière du Douanier Rousseau,* After the Douanier Rousseau, Paris, 1980. (288)

Willy Ronis *La Ciotat,* summer, 1947. (292)

Willy Ronis *Place Vendôme sous la pluie,* The Place Vendôme in the rain, Paris, 1947. (293)

Willy Ronis *Nu de dos,* Back view of nude, May 1955. (297)

Willy Ronis *La péniche aux enfants, sur la Seine,* The children's barge, on the Seine, January 1959. (299)

Emmanuel Sougez *Trois poires,* Three pears, 1934. (305)

Emmanuel Sougez *Blancs,* In White, 1947. (308)

Jean Dieuzaide *Aveyron, Cascade de la Roque* 1981. (317)

Jean-Pierre Sudre *Le panier aux oeufs,* The egg basket, Bouley-Morin, 1953. (310)

Jean Dieuzaide *Feuille de chardon après la pluie,* Thistle leaves after rain, 1978 (316)

Edouard Boubat *Lucette enceinte de Clémence,* Lucette carrying Clémence, 1971 (282)

Patrick Faïgenbaum *Portrait,* 1981. (331)

CONTEMPORARY PHOTOGRAPHY

Photography is both artform and industry. As art it moves towards the outer bounds of creativity, to beyond definition. Yet as industry it can adapt itself well to the bustle of the modern world. Photography as art has had consciously to keep itself distinct from the hurly-burly of the mass, to learn to take itself seriously. Creative photography has been shaped by a series of rebellions. To understand its development one must look at the work of those who rebelled.

In the 1950s subjective and poetic rapportage was the fashion, summed up in Steichen's Museum of Modern Art exhibition, 'Five French Photographers' (as in his later and very influential Family of Man world exhibition), and in the publication of numerous books of photographs, including Izis's *Paris des Rêves*, Doisneau's *Banlieue de Paris*, and Ronis's *Belleville-Ménilmontant*. Cartier-Bresson's *Images à la sauvette* contained his classic definition of photography as the capturing of a decisive moment of reality. This attitude of benevolent distance was confronted by Roland Barthes's criticism of photography for its sentimental humanism and complicity with injustice. Many younger photographers took as their ideal Robert Frank, whose direct vision of grim reality was published in his *Americans* (French edition 1958). Groups such as the XV and the 'Club des 30 x 40', justly the most famous and long-lasting of the Paris photographic societies, were more catholic in their views, accepting Surrealism, for example, while disapproving aesthetics for their own sake. The 1960's in European photography were marked by a growing sense of unease with public and official institutions, an unease that culminated in the events of May 1968. In parallel, the teaching of Otto Steinert in Saarbrucken and later in Essen aimed for 'subjective photography', in which technical mastery of the medium was wedded to a breadth of subject-matter, abstract or avant garde as it might be. In France, after 1968, the Bibliothèque Nationale's own photographic gallery was deliberately separated from the main buildings, opening directly onto the street. The ambiguities of photography, its middle or mean role in the arts, either as between high and low art, or between fine and commercial art - photography as a means of expression for those who do not consider themselves artists - photography as the middle ground - continue to be the subject of critical writing and concern. The Groupe Libre-Expression was a forum for such a debate, through its meetings and exhibitions, until it closed in 1971. For while the events of 1968, dramatic in themselves, led to a reconciliation between political idealisms and plastic realities, freeing photography from sensationalism and manipulation in the process, they also led to a dissolution of some formal groupings, encouraging photographers and artists to seek individual, unaligned roles.

In 1976 Edouard Boubat's *La Survivance* was published by Mércure de France. In this book Boubat wove together rapportage and pure poetry with a marvellous clarity of vision. Gilles Ehrmann's *Faire un pas*, the most beautiful book of photographs in our time, sadly remained as an uncompleted project at the author's home, reflecting the perfectionist and secretive traits of this great artist.

Rapportage, like any other movement, has had its periods of highs and lows. Even when it seemed to be completely out of favour it has resurfaced again, with the lively 'American style', easy to recognise but difficult to define, enduring despite its many different manifestations - a style that married the direct recording of actuality, however passing, of events, trivial or brutal, with exemplary control and virtuosity in taking the photograph itself. To catch the moment when real life becomes art requires more than mere luck. It follows great inner reflection and indeed consideration of the history of photography. There is no longer a 'nature seen through a temperament' but a nature and temperament that are interdependent like two facets of the same work. Looking at the work of Yves Guillot, one has the feeling of the unconscious outside looking in. His works, rather than becoming more and more organised, give an impression of discontinuity.

The city of Paris, under the leadership of Jean-Luc Monterosso, has shown tremendous dynamism in its treatment of contemporary photography. Facilities such as the photography section of the Musée d'Art Moderne de la Ville de Paris and the gallery at Les Halles provide for the medium and the Mois de la Photo, begun in 1976, covers Paris with a diversity of exhibitions each year. However the initiative that has had the greatest influence is the Rencontres Internationales d'Arles which was conceived by Lucien Clergue and the curator Jean-Marie Rouquette. Initially a modest affair when it began in 1970, it has grown to occupy an unique place in world photography, an international competition unrivalled by its many imitators.

The provinces have shown their own vitality in other ways also. Decentralisation, generally more talked of than seen in France, has had some excellent results. Toulouse boasts a number of quality galleries quite apart from the remarkable Municipale Galerie du Chateau d'Eau. In Lyons and Alsace too galleries have been established. Enthusiastic local groups, tired of the rigidity of the amateur circuits, have organised excellent exhibitions, particularly in Brittany and Bordeaux. In Metz, Jean-Luc and Michele Tartarin have set up a centre where far sighted exhibitions are held.

The government has also played its part. In 1978 the first Fondation Nationale was set up in Lyons. In 1982 a Centre Nationale was put in the hands of Robert Delphire and he used to effect the vast exhibition space of the Palais de Tokyo in Paris. He also published a collection of paperbacks called *Photopoche,* which popularised the work of the top professionals. Photographers were also able to work for the government's town and country planning office. In Arles, working in the favourable climate created by the festival, Alain Desvergnes provided an official presence by setting up the Ecole Supérieure de Photographie.

Nowadays prizes and competitions seem a little old-fashioned. However as points of reference and as they are still keenly contested, they have a role to play. In 1984 the Société des Gens d'Image set up the Prix Nièpce and, for books, the Prix Nadar. Such competitions maintain their vitality by adapting as photography adapts. The admission of photography into the competition for the Prix de Rome shows official recognition of the medium.

The multiplicity of manifestations and differing relationships with other artforms make photography a fertile ground for interpretation by critics. It is a sign of photography's coming of age that a number of commentators and theorists have appeared who do not practice photography themselves. This group first made themselves felt at the very beginning of the 1970's. Apart from the critics of exhibitions whose work was necessarily temporal and impressionistic, there were critics who had a more general and philosophic approach. Michael Nuridsany in *Le Figaro* and Patrick Roegiers in *Le Monde* were among the first to establish themselves.

Symptomatic of the new appreciation of photography, the excellent magazine *Chroniques de l'art vivant* devoted a whole issue to photography in 1973. Another avant-garde magazine, *Art Press*, continues to publish many articles on photography by critics such as Régis Durand. However France does not have magazines written by and for the serious enthusiast like England's *Creative Camera*, Germany's *European Photography,* Spain's *Photovision,* Holland's *Perspektief* or Belgium's *Clichés.* Apart from two or three exceptions most photo magazines have more in common with *Playboy* than with the avant-garde. There is, however, *Camera International* which is a beautiful, well-printed album. Sadly *Photographies*, edited by the brilliant Jean-François Chevrier, an historical journal which argued that art can only work together with culture, disappeared all too soon.

Cahiers de la Photographie, founded by Gilles Mora and Claude Nori, sees itself as a theoretical review. It has considered the primary notions of photography as the 'act' of the photographer and as an impression of reality. Among the books published by them have been Henri Vanlier's *La philosophie de la Photographie* in 1983, a thorough re-examination of principles, and Roland Barthes's *La chambre claire* in 1980, a personal exploration having little relevance to the present state of photography.

Much of today's exploration of photography is centred around the position of photography relative to the avant-garde. Photography will take its place as one of the fine arts when the notion of separate arts has gone out of favour. Because it has not established its own identity, photography has been used to bolster other artforms, rather than establishing itself. It is used to express other arts when it should be expressing photography. Christian Boltanski's use of photographs to evidence real life shows how photographs can be used to transmit the artist's concepts. But it also shows that the photographs themselves have their own presence and their own aesthetic autonomy. Boltanski aimed to explore the limits of art and kitsch through the use of photography.

Certain photographers have clearly taken a step towards painting and show their large colour compositions in galleries specialising in painting. George Rousse in particular makes use of painting to render reality ambiguous in his photographs. Similarly Pascal Kern who exalts in the richness of his materials by filling his vast still-lives with objects that have been painted beforehand.

Today's main tendency is the result of the merging of two ideas; photography as *mise en scène* and photography that intensifies the presence of the material. From the union of these two concepts came a fiction-photography that would have been unimaginable a few years ago, taking as it does a make-believe world of the old masters of painting. This movement became possible because photography found, at last, a new form; the depth of shadow, which André Malraux called 'the aquarium of the unreal'. The descriptive shadow became tactile and the tactile mythical. Bernard Faucon, one of the main proponents of the use of *mise en scène*, rendered it twice as artificial by using dummies in a materialisation of his pastel blue dreams. Tom Drahos was one of the first to use *mise en scène*, creating theatres of plasticine and paper. In his hands the device gained depth and expression. Difficult to place, his explosive and unexpected inventions always took the critics by surprise.

The tactile effects of light itself form the subject of Keiichi Tahara's series of *Fenêtres (Windows)*. Indistinctness of image, and minimalism of content, permit the eye to contemplate the very material that constitutes the photograph. Such studies permit the photographer to address the fundamental question of whether the medium of photography does have a substance that can support or contain creativity. Colour photography shares some of these preoccupations, while still because of its different nature remaining apart, concerned with its specific problems: does colour, for example, make the presentation of reality less serious, or can it rather be used to make plays on aspects of fantasy and marvel.

There has only been space here to show and to comment on the work of a few of the contemporary photographers in France. In the main, photography in France today is concerned with interiority: it is far distant from the tradition of rapportage: no more accordions or streetlamps or corner bars and bistros. This intellectual photography, however, is not incorporeal. The escape from the mundane has been towards the substance of photography, as the original source material for its fictive universe. Until recently the defence of photography relied on its very precariousness, so that it could be treated as an open area for experiment and trial amid the fixtures of modern art. But perhaps things are beginning to change. While approaching maturity, photography gains coherence. From now on photography, like the arts of the past, will share common dreams: perhaps this is the price for finally entering the domain of art. But the future of creativity has always eluded speculation.

Jean-Claude Lemagny
Conservateur au Cabinet des estampes de la Bibliothèque Nationale

Alain Fleisher *Happy days with Velasquez,* 1987. (352)

Top and above: **Denis Roche** *22 fevrier 1985. Lougsor,* February 22nd, 1985. Luxor, Egypt. Habou Hotel. (338)

Pierre De Fenoÿl *Alexandria,* June, 1983. (320)

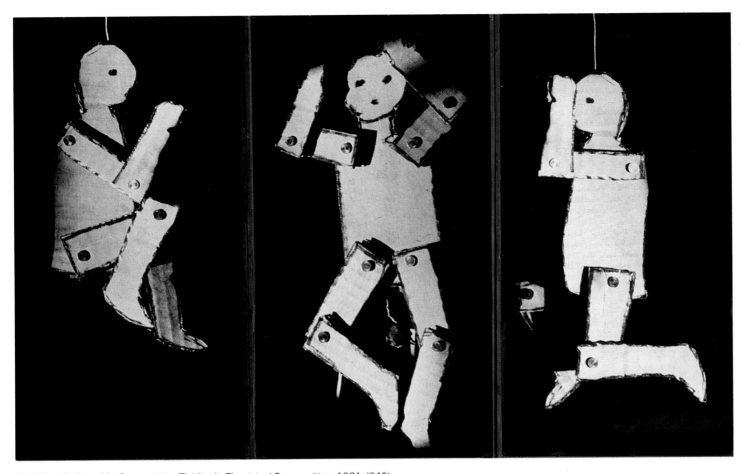

Christian Boltanski *Composition Théâtrale,* Theatrical Composition, 1981. (349)

Patrick Bailly-Maître-Grand *Lune,* Moon, 1985. (353)

Keiichi Tahara *Fenêtre,* Window, 1978. (342)

Pierre De Fenoÿl *Paysage mouillé,* Soaking landscape, 1984. (321)

Bernard Faucon *La neuvième chambre d'amour,* The ninth chamber of love, n.d. (333)

Bernard Faucon *La chambre d'or: le tabernacle,* The chamber of gold: the tabernacle, 1987. (336)

Nancy Pajic-Wilson *Le Cirque: acrobates,* The Circus: acrobats, 1971-83 (348)

Tom Drahos *Papiers froissés,* Crumpled papers, 1982. (327)

Tom Drahos *Papiers froissés,* Crumpled papers, 1982. (326)

Pascal Kern *Fiction colorée,* Fiction in colours, 1985. (354)

Ernest Pignon-Ernest *Rimbaud,* 1978. (355)

George Rousse Untitled, Sommevoir, 1983. (356)

BIOGRAPHIES

The biographies are in the order that artists appear in the catalogue section.

Robert Demachy

Demachy was born, on 7 July 1859, in Saint-Germain en Laye, the third son of Adolphe Demachy, founder of the Demachy bank. In 1882 he became a member of the Sociéte Française de Photographie. It was a further twelve years before he discovered and began to use the gum-bichromate process of printing for which he is best remembered. His first prints were exhibited at the London Photographic Salon and later at the inaugural Exhibition of Photographic Art organised by the Photo-club de Paris. They were an instant success. His first individual exhibition, organised by the Photo-club de Paris, followed in the next year. This established him in the top rank of Pictorialists.

Writing in *Camera Work*, Stieglitz said, 'While he is not the inventor or discoverer of the use of gum-bichromate for photographic printing purposes, he is indisputably the originator of its present use. Taking up an almost forgotten process, his knowledge and genius pointed out its possibilities, and it was he who by his experiments and results blazed out that photographic trail which so many have followed.'

In 1897 Demachy published his first book *Photo-aquatint or the Gum-bichromate Process*. The powerful, ultra conservative Royal Photographic Society exhibited his work in 1901, 1904 and 1907. Many of his photographs were published in *Camera Work*, particularly in 1904. In 1905, together with Stieglitz, he was made an honorary member of the Royal Photographic Society. The British Press welcomed this 'artist of genius' and saw him as a perfect artistic symbol of the political entente cordiale that had just been signed between France and Great Britain.

In 1911 he invented the oil transfer process. He rapidly mastered this complex new technique and exhibited the results at the Societé des Artistes Créateurs des Champs Elysée in March 1911. Three years later however, Demachy gave up photography for good. He never gave any reason for his decision. He did agree nevertheless, to a large retrospective which was held in 1931 and which exhibited his work along with that of his friend Puyo. Demachy died in Hennequeville five years later.
A.S.

E.J.Constant Puyo

Born in 1857, Constant Puyo took up photography as an amateur while an artillery officer. In 1895 he joined the Photo-Club de Paris and in 1896 was admitted to the Linked Ring. Along with Demachy, he rapidly became one of the dominant figures of French Pictorialism. And yet, after World War I, that elegant and sensual art sunk into ready-made formuli of insipid sentimentality.
Constant Puyo died in 1933.
A.S.

Eugène Atget

Eugène Atget was born on 12 February 1857 into a coach-building family at Libourne, near Bordeaux. His parents died soon after and he was brought up by his uncle. After working as a sailor on American liners he became an actor, entering the Conservatoire de Paris in 1879. While touring in minor productions playing bit parts he took up painting and from painting moved to photography. In the 1890s he established himself as a Parisian photographer specialising in street scenes. He captured the fast-disappearing world of Paris' villages with their old shops and small businesses. To avoid the crowds he took to the streets in the early hours; his tall, slightly stooping figure clad in a long, frayed coat weighed down with over fifty pounds of photographic equipment. His clients were lovers of old Paris and artists who admired his work. His prints were bought by libraries, his negatives by the Archives des Monuments Historiques and his albums on chosen subjects (such as Parisian interiors and old signboards) by the Cabinet des Estampes.

From 1914 Atget's output diminished and he spent his time cataloguing his negatives. Although the *Révolution Surréaliste* published four of his photographs in 1926, Atget had, by the time of his death a year later, been completely forgotten. His work was, however, seen by the American photographer Berenice Abbott in Man Ray's studio. With the help of the collector Lucien Levy she was able to save all the negatives and prints that had been abandoned. They are now in the photographic collection of the Museum of Modern Art in New York.

But was Atget an artist in the sense that he was aware of his artistic genius? It has been argued that masterpieces can only be created by conscious acts. Berenice Abbott showed that Atget's images presupposed conscious and deliberate decisions. But Atget certainly never perceived the sense that Surrealists attributed to his photographs; that they were pure objects of irrational fascination. Further, critics, such as Margaret Nesbit, have shown that Atget's work can be explained by his desire to please as many clients as possible. However the school of thought which emphasises personal qualities outside recognised genres sees the depth, truthfulness and documentary investigation of Atget's work as qualifying him as an artist. By no means a naif, he loved to discuss aesthetic matters and would defend his opinions with passion. He never forgot his career as an actor and gave talks on the classical theatre.
J.-C.L.

Brassaï

Born on 9 September 1894 Brassaï took his name from the town in which he was born - Brasso in Hungary. His real name was Gyula Halasz. He studied in Budapest then served in the Austro-Hungarian army in the last two years of the First World War. He completed his studies at the Akademische Hochschule in Berlin in 1921-22. It was on his arrival in Paris in 1924 that he adopted his pseudonym. He was initially interested in drawing and sculpture and turned to photography later. Inspired by the beauty of Paris at night, he photographed everything that captured his attention; faces, streets, landscapes, every kind of human activity. He met Picasso in 1932 through the publisher Tériade and published his first photographs in *Le Minotaure*. He always maintained that his participation in the Surrealist movement was due to a misunderstanding. His photographs were considered Surreal because they showed Paris drowned in darkness and fog, seemingly fantastic and unreal. However he saw them as merely reality rendered fantastic by vision. In 1936 he began his lengthy collaboration with *Harper's Bazaar* which lasted until 1963. He enjoyed great freedom to chose his subjects and photographed many artists. He refused to take any photographs during the war but frequented Picasso's studio. *Conversations With Picasso,* which was not published until 1964, was the result. In 1978 he received the Grand Prix National des Arts. He died in Paris six years later.
A.S.

Jacques-Henri Lartigue

Jacques-Henri Lartigue was born, on 13 June 1894, into a wealthy Courbevoie family. He studied art at the Académie Julian with the painter Jean-Paul Laurens. His paintings were traditional figurative works but the photographs he took possessed far greater life and spontaneity. They evoke a bygone time of ease and pleasure, recorded in lengthy, autobiographical captions. He died in 1987.
A.S.

André Kertèsz

Born on 2 July 1894, in Budapest, Kertèsz went to business school then worked as a stock market account clerk (with a spell in the Austro-Hungarian army on the Polish and Roumanian fronts). He became interested in photography at eighteen but it was not until he settled in France, thirteen years later, that he became a full-time photographer. He took on freelance magazine assignments before joining the staff of *Vu* magazine in 1928. In the same year he married the Hungarian photographer Rogi André. After their divorce five years later, he married Elisabeth Sali. They moved to New York where he took up a job with the Keystone agency. He freelanced again from 1937 to 1949, then spent thirteen years with publishers Condé-Nast, after which he freelanced again.

Critics of the 1960s and 1970s saw Kertèsz as the epitome of the 'modern' photographer. He was one of the first professionals to systematically use a portable camera and he always claimed to be an instinctive photographer. His prolific output was patchy in its quality and 1980s critics may see his deliberate desire to distance himself from the great aesthetic movements of the century as weakening the strength of his work. He died in New York on 28 September 1985.
A.S.

Roger Parry

Born in Paris on 30 November 1905, Parry studied at the Ecole des Beaux-Arts and at the Ecole des Arts Décoratifs. His first job was working for the Galeries Lafayette department store as a stand decorator. In 1929 he spent a year as Maurice Tabard's assistant at the Deberny-Peignot studios. In 1930 his splendid photographs were used as illustrations in L.P. Fargue's *Banalités*. In the years that followed he travelled to Africa and Tahiti as a photo-journalist for the Opera Mundi agency. He also worked for Gallimard publishers and for numerous magazines, including *Vu, Voilá, Jazz* and *Marianne.* During the war he was a war correspondent for Agence France Presse, then returned to Gallimard to work solely on André Malraux's books. He died in Cognac at the age of seventy-two.

Florence Henri

Florence Henri was the child of a French father and German mother. She was born in New York, on 28 June 1883, then spent her young life in Silesia, Paris, Vienna, Rome and Berlin. In Berlin she studied the piano with Ferrucio Busoni from 1911 to 1914. She then became interested in painting and took classes with Kurt Schwitters, first at Berlin's Academy of Fine Arts and then in Munich. In Paris in the mid-twenties she studied with André Lhote, Fernand Léger and Amedée Ozenfant at the Académie Moderne. Finally she took lessons with Moholy-Nagy and Albers at the Bauhaus in Dessau.

Henri then turned to photography. In the large Film und Photo exhibition in Stuttgart in 1929, eighty-one of her photographs were exhibited. A year later she held her first solo exhibition at Studio 28. Exhibitions at the Galerie Xavier Normand, Kunstring Folkwang (Essen) and Galerie de la Pleiade followed. Her photographs appeared in magazines such as *Cercle et Carré, Arts et Metiers Graphiques* and *Art et Décoration*. She also had many commissions for advertising and fashion photography. However in 1938 she gave up photography and returned to painting. She retired in 1963 to the small village of Belleval and died nineteen years later in Compiégne.
A.S.

Robert Bresson

Born on 25 September, 1901 at Brémont-Lamoth in Le Puy de Dome, Robert Bresson received a very classical education at a school near Paris (Lakanal at Sceaux). Bresson frequented the Surrealist circles and devoted himself frenetically to painting and episodically to photography, before making his first film in 1934 *Les Affaires publiques*. He did not make his second film *Les Anges du Péché* until 1943 having spent more than a year as a prisoner of war in Germany. He has since made countless films.
A.S.

Hans Bellmer

Hans Bellmer was born on 13 April 1902 in Katowice, the son of a Silesian mining engineer. Rebelling against the strict discipline imposed by his parents, he ran away to Berlin where he mixed with the Dadaists. He studied drawing with Grosz at the Higher Technical School in the early twenties and then with Otto Dix. He did not meet the Surrealists until 1935.

As a protest against the climate of suspicion engendered by the rise of National Socialism, Bellmer resolved to do no work that could be of use to the State. He began work on a life-sized doll and recorded its creation in photographs. He paid for them to be published by a small printing firm at Karlsruhe in 1934, reprinted in Paris in 1936. He prepared another book, *Les jeux de la poupé*, based on a text by Paul Eluard, which was finally published in 1949. For Bellmer, photography was a means of giving life and reality to his mechanical doll.

In 1938 Bellmer left Berlin for Paris where he lived for the rest of his life. From then on he took photographs only occasionally. In 1945-46 he worked on the illustrations for George Bataille's *L'histoire de l'oeil* and in 1958 his work was used on the cover of *Surréalisme Même*. Bellmer's bursts of photographic activity were sparked by his relationship with the Berlin Surrealists and by his complex relationship with Unica Zoran (who committed suicide in 1970). The period of crisis in 1945-6, after years of wandering, in which he found himself in a 'brutal combat for food and heat, and against lawyers', also stimulated his output. Photography's appeal to Bellmer lay in its immediacy and its capability of expressing his slightest fantasy. However he had little commercial success with it and so turned to drawing and engraving. His photographs with their impression of lightning speed remain among the most powerful produced by Surrealism.
A.S.

Jean Painlevé

Born in Paris in 1902, Jean Painlevé was the son of the mathematician Paul Painlevé, an important political figure in the Third Republic. He first studied medicine but after 1927 devoted himself to scientific film making. His strange and surprising images often appeared in Surrealist publications.
A.S.

Jacques-André Boiffard

Born on 29 July 1902, a native of Epernon, Boiffard was a fellow student of Pierre Naville, the 1924 editor of *La Révolution Surréaliste*. Boiffard was one of the first signatories of the Surrealist Manifesto and one of Man Ray's assistants. He provided the illustrations for André Breton's *Nadja* in 1925, though he was expelled from the Surrealists in 1928. He then founded the Studios Unis with Eli Lotar. Despite the financial backing of Georges-Henri Riviére and the Vicomte de Noailles, the group lasted only three years. In 1933 and again in 1934 he went to Moscow, then travelled the world with Eli Lotar. Boiffard was politically motivated, joining the Communist party in 1927 and becoming a member of the Association of Revolutionary Writers and Artists. In 1935 he resumed the medical studies abandoned ten years previously and spent the rest of his life in practice as a radiologist. He died in Paris in 1961.
A.S.

Raoul Hausmann

Born in Vienna on 12 July 1886, Hausmann travelled at the age of fourteen to Berlin where he studied painting at the Academy of Fine Arts. When he was twenty-six his first treatise was published in *Der Sturm*. Six years later, in 1918, he signed the first Dadaist manifesto with George Grosz and Tristan Tzara in Berlin. In the following year he founded the magazine *Der Dada* with Baader and took part in the first large Dada exhibition. He became

friendly with Kurt Schwitters in 1920 and soon after switched from painting to photo-montage. In the early thirties many of his photographs and articles appeared in the photography and cinema magazine *A bis Z*. He left Germany in 1933 to travel in Spain and France. He lived in Paris from 1938 until 1944, then moved to Limoges where he spent the rest of his life and where he died on 1 February 1971.
A.S.

Erwin Blumenfeld

Born in Berlin on 26 January 1897, Blumenfeld was an active member of the Dada movement from 1918 to 1921. He took up photography after the leather-goods factory he had founded in Amsterdam in 1923 went bankrupt. In 1936 he went to Paris and his highly Surrealistic works were published in *Verve* and *Photo*. *Harper's Bazaar* hired him in 1939 and he became the most sought after post-war fashion photographer. He died in Rome, in after completing his memoirs, *Jadis et Daguerre*, said to have 'a lucid and bitter cruelty'.
A.S.

Man Ray

Emmanuel Rudnitzky was born in Philadelphia on 27 August 1890. He moved to New York and worked in various jobs, taking evening classes at the city's National Academy of Design in 1908 and later at the Ferrer School from 1911 to 1913. There he produced his first abstract work, *Tapestry*, in 1911, and struck up a friendship with Alfred Stieglitz. In 1913 he married Adon Lacroix and they moved to an artists' community in New Jersey. He was invited to exhibit in the Armory Show of 1913 but refused. Instead his first exhibition took place at the Daniel Gallery in 1915. In that year he returned to New York where he met Marcel Duchamp and began his first photographic experiments. In 1917, with Duchamp and Picabia, he founded the New York Dada group. The first and last issue of *New York Dada* was published in 1921.
On 14 July 1921, leaving behind his New York studio, Man Ray landed in Le Havre. In December of that year he exhibited his work at the Librarie 6, thanks to Philippe Soupault, a friend of Duchamp. In the following year he rediscovered the technique of photogrammes without cameras which he christened 'Rayographs'. His first album of 12 Rayographs, with a preface by Tristan Tzara, was published under the title *Les Champs Delicieux*. He showed his first film *Rétour à la raison*, in 1923 on the very night of *Le Coeur à Barbe* that marked the end of the Dada movement.

He worked as a fashion photographer, particularly for Paul Poiret, and as a society portraitist. He was also involved in all the activities of the Surrealist group. He made three experimental films; *Emak Bakia* in 1926, *L'étoile de mer* (based on a poem by Robert Desnos) in 1928 and *Les mystéres du chateau du Dé* (commissioned by the Vicomte de Noailles) in 1929, and took

part in numerous exhibitions. Several of his assistants became famous, among them Berenice Abbott, Jacques-André Boiffard, Lee Miller and Bill Brandt. In 1940 Man Ray fled occupied France for Hollywood, where he painted and taught photography at the Art Center School. In 1946 he married Juliet Browner and did not return to Paris until 1951. In 1972 the Musée National d'Art Moderne supported his work by holding a large retrospective.

He died in Paris on 18 November 1976.
A.S.

Maurice Tabard

Born in Lyons on 19 July 1897, Tabard studied the violin with little success before moving to New Jersey, where his father had gone to work in the silk factories. He studied at the New York Institute of Photography from 1918 to 1922, then worked for six years as an assistant at Bachrach's portrait studio. In 1930 he moved to Paris and worked at the Deberney-Peignot studio for a year. Thereafter he took photographs for fashion and advertising. His work was also published in magazines such as *Bifur* and *Photographie* and exhibited in the Modern European Photograph Exhibition (organised by Julian Levy in New York) and in the annual exhibitions of the Galerie La Pleiade (1931-34).

During the war, Tabard worked for Gaumont as a studio photographer, then as a war correspondent. Afterwards he returned to fashion photography working for *Harper's Bazaar* in New York from 1946-48, then returning to Paris where he worked for numerous magazines. He died in Nice aged eighty-seven. Tabard was a prolific photographer and a remarkable technician. His work tended to become increasingly formalist even though still in elegant style.
A.S.

Raoul Ubac

Born on 22 March 1910 in Malmedy, Belgium, Ubac first came into contact with the Surrealists while he was studying at the School of Applied Arts in Cologne. Settling in Paris in 1934, he took part in all the movement's activities until the beginning of he war. The Surrealists, he wrote, 'held that all techniques were valid, so long as they were the means of bringing certain profound revelations to light. For my part, I adopted photography, which technically fascinated me much more than drawing or painting, as a means of revealing reality through a succession of unexpected aspects.' For Ubac, this meant destroying the appearance of reality by the random use of different techniques that he found to hand (such as photomontage or solarisation). If necessary, he invented techniques such as petrification which thickens the surface of a print to resemble a bas-relief, or burning, which destroys the gelatin of the negative to reveal a latent image beneath 'the aspect of things'. These experiments were enthusiastically received by the Surrealists, and his photographs accompanied articles in *Minotaure* by Breton, Peret, Mabille and

Eluard.

Yet he had the feeling that he had reached the limits of 'a machine created simply to register reality', and together with this the war 'which took over some of the visionary aspects of Surrealism to restore them as actual horrors, in tragic mood', led Ubac to free himself from Surrealism. Left to his own resources, a refugee in Carcassonne, Ubac gave up photography in 1945. He then followed a very successful career as a painter and died at Dieudonné on his birthday forty years later.
A.S.

Henri Cartier-Bresson

Henri Cartier-Bresson was born in 1908 into a wealthy textile family from the north of France. He did not obtain a university degree, preferring instead to read forbidden but essential authors such as: Joyce, Proust, Céline and André Breton. Inspired by the memory of an uncle who was a painter, he entered André Lhote's studio. Cartier-Bresson was attracted by Lhote's plastic rigour but rejected his dogmatism.

Drawn by adventure, he lived as a hunter in Africa but due to illness returned to Europe where he took up photography which appealed to him as an accelerated form of drawing. His work was soon published and exhibited and extensive travel in Spain and Mexico supplied fresh subjects.

In 1935 he moved to the cinema, working with Paul Strand and Jean Renoir. In 1940 he was taken prisoner but managed to escape in 1943 and became a portrait photographer of artists and writers. He recorded the Liberation and the return of the French deportees. In 1946, the Museum of Modern Art, believing him dead, prepared a posthumous exhibition of his work. In 1952 he wrote the preface to *Images a la Sauvette* at the request of the editor Tériade, in which he defined his conception of photography in a remarkably clear way.

To prevent him from retreating into 'a precious and mannered Surrealism', his friend Robert Capa hired him as a photo-journalist. It was with Capa, David Seymour and George Rodger that he founded the cooperative photo agency Magnum in 1947, with the aims of protecting the profession from those of purely mercenary instinct. Although a convinced libetarian, he acknowledged the necessary commercialism of art saying, 'one is a photographer in the same way as one is a chair repairer'. His classic book *Flagrants délits*, published in 1968, was the outcome of his travels in the Far East, India and the Soviet Union and was only one of the many books of his work published. In 1966 he left the Magnum Agency, desiring above all to draw. Although he loved to take photographs, he could live without doing so.

Looking at Cartier-Bresson's peers, one might find Walker Evans more profound, Kertèsz (whom he admitted to be his main influence) more sensitive, Robert Frank more modern or Bill Brandt more grand. But Cartier-Bresson is without argument the greatest composer photography has known. Today young photographers hold him in the sort of esteem once accorded to Victor Hugo. At once practical and artistic, Cartier-Bresson knew how to keep out anything that interfered with his passion to compose images. He was able to skilfully work within the constraints of his profession and yet to transcend his art. Interviewed by Gilles Mora, Cartier-Bresson said, 'My vision sweeps across life perpetually. I feel very close to Proust when he says that, 'life, real life finally rediscovered, is literature'.'For me it was photography.'
J.-C.L.

Robert Doisneau

Born in Gentilly in the Val de Marne on 14 April 1912, Doisneau became André Vigneau's photographic assistant at nineteen. His work with Vigneau made him very aware of the importance of light, indeed he attested that, 'happiness on earth is to feel accepted in the great creation of light.' From 1934 he took fashion, advertising, architectural and industrial photographs. He also took shots of 'real people', the people of his Gentilly upbringing. He joined the Rapho agency in 1946 and his work took on great compassion and sensitivity. He said that it was important 'to first like, then to record'.

Doisneau worked with several authors, such as Blaise Cendrars, Jacques Prévert, André Hardelet and Maurice Baquet, to produce books such as *La banlieue de Paris* (1949), *Instantanés de Paris* (1958), *Ballade pour violoncelle* and *Chambre noire* (1981). He continues to capture the world around him with a clear but forgiving eye, with precision but with compassion, and always with great humility. His strong belief is that 'to suggest is to create, to describe is to destroy'.
A de G.S.C.

William Klein

William Klein was born in New York in 1928. He first studied sociology but after military service in Europe was able to obtain a grant to study painting at Fernand Léger's studio. He initially used photography in the fifties for experiments in abstraction in which he slid a luminous brush over the sensitive surface of photographic paper. In 1954 he returned home. *New York* was the result of his photographic rediscovery of the city. It was published at the insistence of the French photographer Chris Marker of Editions du Seuil, in 1956. Klein rapidly achieved recognition for his boldly plastic and insolently inventive fashion photographs for *Vogue*.

Meanwhile he continued researching into the concept of the modern city. *Rome* was published in 1960, followed by *Tokyo* and *Moscow* in 1964. In 1959 he made his first film *On the lights of Broadway* and by the early sixties left photography for the cinema, achieving fame with films such as *Who are you Polly Magoo?* and *Mr. Freedom*.

Klein always took photographs with a book in mind. His interest in graphics led him to take special care with the layout of those books. He was inspired by the blaring typefaces used in the sensational press, 'I wanted to do something perfectly vulgar.' The obvious crudeness and roughness of his photographs, blurred, grainy and full of movement, outraged some critics. They did not see, however, Klein's meticulous, almost manic supervision of the printing of his work which guaranteed that every print was reproduced to his exacting standards.

'I very consciously did the opposite of what was already being done. I thought that things off-centre, at random, subject to accident, from a different angle, would allow the liberation of the photographic image – the camera is capable of surprising us, we must help it.'

Like Robert Frank, Klein aimed to take photographs that were 'just as incomprehensible as life'. But whereas Frank seemed to neglect form, Klein magnified visual effects (although neither forgot reality). Frank destroyed the hierarchies of sense whereas Klein upset the established rules.
J.-C.L.

Izis

Israelis Bidermanas, known as Izis, was born in Mariample, Lithuania, on the 17 January 1911, and moved to Paris in 1930 where he opened his own studio in the 13th Arrondisement. On the outbreak of war he went as a refugee to the area near Limoges, making his living retouching photographs for local professional photographers. In 1944 he joined the F.F.I., making a number of portraits of his fellow maquisards.

On his return to Paris in 1946 he exhibited these and other portraits, together with his views of Paris, which received considerable praise. He came to meet Paul Eluard, Aragon and Breton, as well as other photographers, including Brassaï, Sougez, Kertèsz and Cartier-Bresson. In 1949 he began working for *Paris-Match*, an association that was to last twenty years. Led by his fascination with the relationship between text and image, and with the encouragement of the poet Jacques Prévert, Izis worked on a book about Paris, asking Henry Miller, André Breton and Paulhan to write texts. *Paris des rêves*, published in 1949, was an immediate success. In 1951 he worked with Prévert on another book on the Paris they both so much admired, *Le grand bal du Printemps*, and in 1952 they published *Les charmes de Londres*. In the same period Izis worked with Colette on a book on nature, *Le paradis terrestre*. In 1955 his *Israel*, with a foreword by Malraux, appeared. Other books include *Le cirque* (with Prévert), *Le monde de Chagall*, and *Paris des poètes* (1977).

Izis, who died in Paris in 1980, disliked artifice. While only recording what pleased him, he never posed his photographs or set up scenes: he avoided even being seen by his subjects.
A de G.S.C.

Edouard Boubat

Born in Paris in 1923, Boubat studied photoengraving at the Estienne school and took photographs for pleasure. In 1947 he received first prize at the Salon National and by that time had taken the photo that became his motif, *la Petite fille aux feuilles mortes*. The photograph shows a little girl, sad and alone, who has been left or forgotten in the Luxembourg gardens. He turned professional, met Robert Frank and Eugene Smith and, in 1951, Bertie Gilou. Gilou was the artistic director of *Realités* and brought Boubat onto the magazine's staff along with Jean Philippe Charbonnier and Giles Ehrmann. In that year, Boubat exhibited with Robert Doisneau at the La Hune bookshop-gallery, one of the few places to support photography at that time.

Boubat travelled the world taking photographs. Wherever he went, however, he created his own environment, an environment of calm and beauty. His work is easily recognised. He became known as 'correspondent of peace', a title given him by Jacques Prévert. In 1973 Boubat's friend, the novelist Michel Tournier wrote, 'Boubat's landscapes all have something of that divine regard placed like a benediction at the end of a day of creation. Faced with his images the word grace comes to mind and it is difficult to know whether it should be used in its theological or choreographic sense, such is the inseparability of the beauty of the gesture and the goodness of heaven.' Amongst his numerous books *Survivance,* published by Mercure de France, in 1976 deserves special mention.
J.-C.L.

Willy Ronis

Born in Paris in 1910 Ronis was the son of a professional photographer. He first studied drawing and music but joined his father's studio in 1932, taking over four years later. He worked as a freelance photo-journalist in Paris, throughout France and in the Balkans. His work was used by the French tourist office and French railways. During the war he took several jobs in the south of France. After the Liberation, he returned to Paris and became part of the Groupe des XV which counted Sougez, Jahan, René-Jacques and Masclet amongst its members. In 1947 Ronis received the Kodak prize, in 1957 he was awarded the gold medal in the Venice Biennial and in 1979 he was given the Grand Prix National.

Ronis published his first book in 1951. But he is best known for *Belleville-Ménilmonant* published three years later. It is one of the great photo-essays of Paris, alongside those of Izis, Doisneau and Brassaï. In 1981 he received the Prix Nadar for his book *Sur le fil du hasard*. Ronis was one of the first people to elevate the teaching of photography in France above a very basic level. He did most of his teaching at the University of Provence.

Although Ronis admired innovation in the work of others, he preferred to confine his own work to familiar, everyday subjects. To those he applied great care; he liked, he said, to perch himself 'on the edge of the daisies', watching for the moment to arrive.
J.-C.L.

Emmanuel Sougez

A native of Bordeaux, born in 1889, Sougez's first interests were painting and art history and he studied them first at the Ecole des Beaux-Arts, then at Bordeaux University. After graduation in 1911 he went to Paris where he soon gave up painting for photography. He said that he 'preferred to be a good photographer, rather than a bad painter'. He had taken photographs since he was thirteen, but he really learnt his craft working alongside foreign photographers in Switzerland and Germany. In 1926 he was asked to set-up and oversee the photographic section of *Illustration* magazine. This became the centre of French photography for a time.

Sougez's influence was felt in many areas. He introduced modern processes such as colour photography, worked with authors such as Raymond Lécuyer and Peter Polack to produce books on photographic history, brought together authentic creative French photographers into a group called Rectangle (which later became the Groupe des XV) and published the work of the best new French and foreign photographers in *Arts et Métiers Graphiques* between 1930 and 1939.

After the war he earned his living by photographing the work of interior designers. Sougez's photographs can be divided into his professional and his experimental work. The former include landscapes, photo-journalistic pieces and reproductions of art (some, such as the photographs of Rodin's sculptures, are works of art themselves). The latter are a series of still-lives, made on negatives measuring 30 x 40 cm. They have a luminous and pure quality. His best work is now in public collections.

He died in Paris on 24 August 1972.
J.-C.L.

Jean-Pierre Sudre

A native Parisian, Sudre was born on 27 September 1921. He studied film-making for several years before exhibiting his photographic work in 1952. The exhibition catalogue contained a foreword by Brassaï. From 1957 onwards Sudre put together hundreds of photography books, containing unique or limited edition prints, for large industrial firms. In the early sixties he was among the first to lobby for the recognition of photography as a means of creative expression. From 1965 to 1970 he taught at the Ecole Superieure d'Architecture and at the Cambre in Brussels. He set up the Photography Department at the Ecole Superieure d'Arts Graphiques in Paris between 1968-72. In 1973 he moved to Lacoste with his wife Claudine. Here they hold annual photography seminars. Sudre is an alchemist who, in the darkness of his laboratory, guides the development of living light under the light of his enlarger. At all times he is the director dazzled by his own ability to reveal to us the secret life of seemingly mundane objects.
A. de G.S.C.

Jean Dieuzaide

Dieuzaide was born in Grenade sur Garonne on 20 June 1921. He became a reporter, photographing the liberation of Toulouse at the end of the war. He was South-West correspondent for *Paris Match*, *Parisien Libéré* and for various sports papers. In 1950 he gave up journalism for publishing and travelled through Spain and Portugal capturing images of great pathos. In the mid-fifties, Zodiaque Editions published his photographs in a series of twelve books on Romanesque Art and Editions Arthaud used his work to illustrate books on topology. When back in Toulouse he began taking the experimental industrial and scientific photographs which intrigued him for a further thirty years.

While working on commissioned pieces he was also able to pursue his interest in still-life, an area in which he was greatly influenced by Sougez. His output was prodigious: many of the 500,000 archived photographs have never been exhibited.

Dieuzaide worked tirelessly to promote photography, defending notions of photographic quality and the use of original prints. He headed the first municipal gallery of photography in France, the Chateau d'Eau in Toulouse, opened by him in 1974.
A. de G.S.C.

Christian Boltanski

Boltanski was born in Paris on 6 September 1944. At fourteen he had already decided that he 'wanted to paint and make art'. From 1976 onwards, however, he was a painter who used photography and nothing else. Before that he used photography to examine photography's stereotypes, whether in his childhood (in *10 Photographic portraits of Christian Boltanski*) or in reality through a series of pedestrian images (in *Model Images*, 1968). In 1976 Boltanski began a series of compositions of everyday objects. He assembled and photographed them without visual reference and blew them up to achieve definitive pictorial reality. His Japanese compositions of 1980, fairy-like tinselly images of the Far East, are superb proof that 'one can be a painter without using a paintbrush'.
A.S.

Pierre de Fenoÿl

De Fenoÿl, a native of Paris, was born in 1945. He began his career working for other photographers as an archivist, first in 1966 for Henri Cartier-Bresson, then, in 1969, for the Magnum agency. In 1970, together with Charles Henri Favrod and Rencontre publishers, he set up the first private photographic gallery in Paris. Five years later, his all-round knowledge of photography, including its problems, made him a very youthful Director of the Fondation Nationale de la Photographie. This institution aimed to promote and coordinate photographic creativity. When the Pompidou Center opened in 1977, de Fenoÿl became coordinator of photographic activities there. In 1982 he published *Les chefs d'oeuvre des photographes anonymes*, a radical work questioning established dogma on the history of creative photography.

From 1980 onward, another Pierre de Fenoÿl appeared - the artist. He was regarded as an amateur until his trips to Italy and Egypt. Then his eye, trained over the years, showed itself to be one the of the most powerful of his generation. His true worth as a photographer was seen in the 1984 Exhibition of his work held at the Musée National d'Art Moderne. He then moved to the South of France where he took powerful but subtle landscapes. These were exhibited at the Bibliothéque Nationale in 1987. He also managed to save the phototype process by preserving one of the last working studios before his untimely death, from a heart attack, in 1987.
J.-C.L.

Tom Drahos

Tom Drahos was born in Jablon Czecholovakia on 17 November 1942. He studied photography at the School of Graphic Arts in Prague and then took classes at the Academy of Cinema before going to Paris where he enrolled at the Institute of Higher Studies in Cinema from 1969-1972. Drahos's early work was in the field of reportage, but he rapidly and radically turned his back on this profession in order to devote his energy exclusively to research of a constant and unsettling inventiveness. Given a comission to photograph the Parisian suburbs by the Délégation a l'Aménagement du Territore (Urban and Land Planning) Drahos 'played on the choice of filters in order to produce harsh coloured monochromes; he mounted the elements that consisted of torn pieces of photographs stapled together, treated like tiles or stained glass, broken fragments of glass or old papers. He then arranged them in the form of abstact 'signs' or as vast panoramic miniatures. This treatment of familiar places (charged with strong emotional and ideological connotations) no doubt raised eyebrows. However it is coherent with the idea that one might have of representation today - with photography or beyond it.'
A.S.

Patrick Faïgenbaum

Faïgenbaum was born in Paris in 1954. His first interests were painting (which he took up at fifteen) and jazz. He began taking photographs in 1973. His most significant early influence was Bill Brandt, whom he met in London in 1974. Other influences were Richard Avedon and Diane Arbus. In 1977 he visited the United States where he was impressed with the work of W. Eugene Smith and Ralph Gibson.

He supported himself by working as a salesman in a Paris camera shop until, in 1984, a grant enabled him to live in Florence. There he undertook a series of photographs of the Italian upper classes in their home environment. In 1985 he received the Prix de Rome which allowed him to spend two years at the Villa Medicis. There he took photographs of the top Roman families, placing them in front of their tapestries and Old Masters. There they stand, stiff and formal, conscious of their great lineage but radiating intense presence, a presence that is just as strong as that of Sander's middle classes or Arbus' outsiders.
J.-C.L.

Bernard Faucon

Bernard Faucon offers one of the most beautiful examples of a photographer capable of communicating a private universe. Born in 1950 at Apt-en-Provence he studied at the local schools before entering the Sorbonne where he studied philosophy until 1973. But having decided to model his life on his dreams he also took up painting. His paintings on the theme of children in water – large diluted spaces out of which concrete figures loom – led him to photography. The film maker Jean-Claude Larrieu initiated him to the technique. Making use of shop-window dummies – little boys with empty stares and stiff gestures – Faucon posed them in settings and reconstructed intense poetic movements that until now had remained hidden deep within himself. His first exhibition at the ephemeral Galerie Lop Lop in 1977 revealed his work to the public, but it was the 1979 exhibition at the Galerie Agathe Gaillard and the unexpected success at Castelli Graphics in New York that set off his international renown. In the same year he was awarded the Prix de la Ville de Paris for the maquette of his first book *Les Grandes Vacances*.

Faucon meticulously sets up an encompassing space and peoples it with dummies that have been carefully arranged in order to recreate a moment of poetic mystery. He does not hesitate to bring in the elements; water, fire or wind. He takes all the time that is necessary. But nothing exists except for the moment photographed and the presence of a dreamy image in pale colours... both plausible and impossible, pure and perverse. From the beginning his oeuvre has been worked on by the tension between the depth and transparency of the space and its peopling by the unsettling presence of dummies. In the series *Chambres d'Amours* the area itself, empty but haunted, has become poetry throughout.
J.-C. L.

Alain Fleisher

Born on 10 January 1944 in Paris, Fleisher studied modern literature then, on graduation in 1970, worked as a film-maker, artist and photographer. He was a professor at the Ecole Nationale d'Art at Nice from 1976 to 1978 and, from 1979, at the Ecole Nationale d'Art at Cergy. Fleisher has always been fascinated by the use of mirrors where the images dissolve in designed and complex plays of reflections.
A.S.

Patrick Bailly-Maitre-Grand

Bailly-Maitre-Grand was born in Paris on 1 February 1945. He initially studied science, then switched to painting. He first became fascinated in photography in 1979 and since that time has focused his interest on daguerreotypes.

A.S.

Pascal Kern

Born on 13 June 1952 in Paris, Kern studied painting and then began making a series of models of a hypothetical factory cluttered with objects. The *Usine à Bastos (Factory of Bastos)* was exhibited at the Musée National d'Art Moderne in 1980. Since 1982 Kern has worked exclusively with photography. His photographs faithfully record his manipulation of objects which he has presented in their natural size, with a frontal viewpoint and in natural light.

A.S.

Denis Roche

Roche was born in Paris in 1937, but lived until he was nine in Venezuela and Brazil, before returning there. He first studied Classics then went to medical school. In 1962 he left to become a member of the direction committee of the literary magazine *Tel Quel*, publishing his first article on the Amazon that year. He became an editor for Tchou publishers (from 1969 to 1970) and then for Le Seuil. He has published numerous articles on photography including *Legendes de Denis Roche, essai photo-autobiographie* in 1982, *La disparution des lucioles* in 1982, *Conversation avec le temps* in 1985 and contributed to *Les Cahiers de la photographie*, a trimestrial journal of photographic criticism and theory.

A.S.

Keiichi Tahara

Tahara was born in Kyoto in 1951. His interest in photography came from his grandfather who was a professional photographer. He studied decoration and cinema at university and then travelled to Paris in 1972 as the lighting engineer for the Red Buddha theatre group. He decided to stay in France, impressed by the light of European skies. His work, with its violent contrasts of light, shows the expressionist influence of compatriots Ikko Narahara and Eikoh Hosoe and the plastic force of William Klein. His first series of photographs of Paris was exhibited at the Bibliothéque Nationale in 1974. His fame eventually spread to his own country, after many years of little recognition, and he received several important commissions. These included the colour illustration of a six volume series on Modern Style architecture throughout the world.

He continued with his own work at the same time and his series entitled *Fenêtres (Windows)*, completed in 1978, is one of the most beautiful achievements in contemporary photography. Tahara accentuates the dust on the windows in a manner that gives the light a sensual presence. In 1980 he continued to explore the explosions and reverberations of light in a series called *Eclats*. His portraits of artists and writers have a broad and bold style. A book of ten years of his creative work in black and white photograph was published in 1984.

J.-C.L.

George Rousse

Born on 28 July 1947 Rousse, a native Parisian, was professionally trained as a photographic technician. At the beginning of the 1980s he became intrigued by the Figuration Libre movement of young French artists. Delighted with their 'lack of complexes' he began painting large figures and faces on the walls, stairways and ceilings of derelict buildings. After the buildings were demolished, the photographs he took of the paintings remain the only permanent record of his art. The work he carried out after this involved complicated and artificial volumes that use and elude all the artifices of perspective.

A.S.

Ernest Pignon-Ernest

Born in Nice in 1924 into modest background, Ernest Pignon-Ernest entered an architectural firm upon the completion of his secondary schooling at the age of 15. He met the members of the Niçoise faction of the group Fluxus and, once his military service was finished, was encouraged by the artist, Ben to take up part-time painting. From 1968 onward his works became increasingly politicized. Life drawings of Rimbaud, very elaborately conceived, were placed in 'situations'- on the walls of public places in the hope that 'they will create new imaginary or real relationships' within another society. Thus 'one day in May, Rimbaud donned his vagabond's clothing...(his) face pasted in decors of ruins or in the midst of red and white traffic signs' and whose only surviving trace is the photograph.

A.S.

Nancy Pajic-Wilson

Pajic-Wilson was born in Perou, Indiana in 1941. She studied literature and art history at university and took a diploma at New York's Cooper Union. She began using photography in 1966 to record the things that she made and as part of her pictorial work. She settled in Paris in 1978 to research techniques that integrate old printing processes in a purely pictorial procedure.

A.S.

PICTORIALISM

1 (see back cover)
Robert Demachy
Nu
Nude, n.d.
Crayon tinted transfer print, 17 x 11
Royal Photographic Society, Bath

2
Figure study, 1906
Gum print, 21.8 x 15.2
Royal Photographic Society, Bath

3
The wind, n.d.
Oil transfer print, 12 x 17
Royal Photographic Society, Bath

4
La Seine
The Seine, n.d.
Oil transfer print, 27 x 19.2
Royal Photographic Society, Bath

2

15

The title shown *in italics* is either the
artist's original title or description or the
short title under which the photograph is
catalogued. Place names and dates are
included in the translation unless they
form part of the original title.

3

4

5 (page 19)
Robert Demachy
Perplexité
Perplexity, n.d.
Oil transfer print, 16.1 x 10.5
Royal Photographic Society, Bath

6 (page 21)
Timide
The timid one, n.d.
Transfer print, 18.2 x 9.6
Royal Photographic Society, Bath

7
Nu
Nude, n.d.
Oil transfer print, 14.6 x 9
Royal Photographic Society, Bath

8
Buste
Bust, n.d.
Oil transfer print, 8.7 x 8.3
Royal Photographic Society, Bath

9
On the Seine, 1906/7
Oil transfer print, 16.5 x 22.5
Royal Photographic Society, Bath

10
Le Panthéon, n.d.
Gum print, 20.8 x 12.3
Royal Photographic Society, Bath

11
Speed, n.d.
Gum print, 15.2 x 23.6
Royal Photographic Society, Bath

12 (page 20)
Souvenir no 2, n.d.
Oil transfer print
Royal Photographic Society, Bath

13 (not illustrated)
Nu
Nude, n.d.
Oil transfer print, 21.8 x 16.2
Royal Photographic Society, Bath

14 (page 18)
Désespoir
Despair, n.d.
Oil transfer print, 14.7 x 14.7
Royal Photographic Society, Bath

15
Nu
Nude,n.d.
Oil transfer print, 14.6 x 9
Royal Photographic Society, Bath

7

8

9

10

11

16
Constant Puyo
Plein-air
In the open air, (between 1894 and
1902)
Albumen print, 23.4 x 16.3 (reference
album)
Coll: Michele Chomette

17
Untitled, (between 1894 and 1902)
Carbon print, 19.9 x 14.7
Coll: Michele Chomette

18
Untitled, n.d.
Albumen print, 23.7 x 14.2
Coll: Michele Chomette

19 (page 23)
Untitled, (between 1894 and 1902)
Bichromate gum print, 22.1 x 9.8
Mounted on grey cardboard
Coll: Michele Chomette

20
Nu
Nude (between 1894 and 1902)
Albumen print, 24.2 x 16.5 (reference
album)
Coll: Michele Chomette

21 (not illustrated)
Portrait, about 1906
Bichromate gum print in four colours,
28.4 x 22.4
Coll: Michele Chomette

22
Portrait, about 1906
Bichromate gum print, 28.6 x 22.5
Coll: Michele Chomette

23
Untitled, (between 1894 and 1902)
Albumen print, 23.3 x 13.4 (reference
album)
Coll: Michele Chomette

24
Untitled, (betwen 1894 and 1902)
Albumen print, 23.3 x 13.4 (reference
album)
Coll: Michele Chomette

16

20

17

18

22

25
Constant Puyo
Untitled, 1912
Gum print, 8.2 x 11
Royal Photographic Society, Bath

26
Effet de lumière
Effect of light, 1898
Exhibited in Budapest in 1903, *Revue
Photographique,* 1903, p. 352
Fresson print, 20.5 x 26.8
Coll: Michele Chomette

27 (page 17)
Sans titre (devant la cheminée)
Untitled (by the fire), 1899
Oil transfer print
Coll: Michele Chomette

28 (page 22)
L'atelier du photographe, rue de Turin
The photographer's studio, rue de Turin,
1924 (chosen by the photographer to
illustrate how to compose a portrait)
Oil transfer print
Coll: Michele Chomette

29
Untitled, n.d.
Silver print, 21.5 x 16.5
Coll: Michele Chomette

30 (page 13)
Tête de Gorgone
Gorgon's head, (between 1894 and
1902)
Albumen print, 23.1 x 16.1
Coll: Michele Chomette

24

23

25

26

RAPPORTAGE I

31
Eugène Atget
Facteur
Postman, 1898
Gold chloride print, 21.7 x 16.5
Coll: B.N., Paris

32
Marchand d'abat-jour, rue Lepic
Lampshade seller, Paris, 1898
Gold chloride print, 21.4 x 17.3
Coll: B.N., Paris

33 (page 29)
Marchand de parapluies
Umbrella vendor, 1898
Gold chloride print, 21.4 x 17.3
Coll: B.N., Paris

34
Boulanger
Baker, 1898
Gold chloride print, 22.2 x 17.1
Coll: B.N., Paris

35
Marchand d'herbes
Herb vendor, 1898
Gold chloride print, 21.4 x 17.3
Coll: B.N., Paris

36
La Butte aux Cailles, Paris, before 1900
Gold chloride print, 16.9 x 21.2
Coll: B.N., Paris

31

32

35

36

37
Eugène Atget
Le pont Marie, Paris
Print made in 1977 by Pierre Gassmann,
22.8 x 17.2
Coll: B.N., Paris

38
Chateau de Bagatelle, Neuilly, n.d.
Print made in 1977 by Pierre Gassmann,
21.2 x 17.4
Coll: B.N., Paris

39
Parc de Sceaux, n.d.
Print made in 1977 by Pierre Gassmann,
23.1 x 17.4
Coll: B.N., Paris

40 (page 31)
Moulin á Charenton
Mill at Charenton, n.d.
Print made in 1977 by Pierre Gassmann,
21.2 x 17.4
Coll: B.N., Paris

41
Arc boutant de l'église Saint Séverin
Buttress, St Séverin's church, Paris, n.d.
Print made in 1977 by Pierre Gassmann,
23.2 x 17.4
Coll: B.N., Paris

42 (page 30)
Roulotte, porte d'Italie
Travelling cart, porte d'Italie, Paris, 1912
Gold chloride print, 21.7 x 17.3
Coll: B.N., Paris

43
Cariole, porte de Choisy
Cart, porte de Choisy, Paris, 1912
Gold chloride print, 16, 9 x 12, 4
Coll: B.N., Paris

44
Le 24-26 rue Sainte Foy, Paris, n.d.
Print made in 1977 by Pierre Gassmann,
17.4 x 23.1
Coll: B.N., Paris

45
*Marchand de chaussures, marché des
Carmes, place Maubert*
Shoe-seller, place Maubert, Paris, n.d.
Gold chloride print, 21, 6 x 16,7
Coll: B.N., Paris

46
Roulotte, porte d'Ivry
Travelling cart, porte d'Ivry, Paris, 1912
Gold chloride print, 16.9 x 21.8
Coll: B.N., Paris

37

38

39

41

40

43

45

46

135

47
Eugène Atget
Roulotte, porte de Montreuil
Travelling cart, porte de Montreuil, 1913
Gold chloride print, 16.8 x 21.7
Coll: B.N., Paris

48 (page 31)
*Hangar de l'auberge du Compas d'Or,
rue Montorgueil*
Cart-shed at the Compas d'Or inn, Paris,
n.d.
Print made in 1977 by Pierre Gassmann,
17.2 x 23.1
Coll: B.N., Paris

49
*Au Petit Bacchus, 61 rue Saint Louis en
L'Ile, Paris,* n.d.
Gold chloride print, 21.3 x 16.9
Coll: B.N., Paris

50
L'atelier du photographe
The photographer's studio, 1912
Gold chloride print, 21,5 x 17,0
Coll: B.N., Paris

51
Boutique de friture, 38 rue de Seine
Food shop, Paris, 1912
Gold chloride print, 21. 4 x 16. 9
Coll: B.N., Paris

52
Au France-Pinot, quai de Bourbon, Paris,
n.d.
Gold chloride print, 21.3 x 16.7
Coll: B.N., Paris

53
*Au Griffon, 39 quai de l'Horloge,
Paris,* n.d.
Gold chloride print, 21.7 x 17.3
Coll: B.N., Paris

54
Le marché des Carmes, place Maubert
The Carmes marketplace, Paris, 1912
Gold chloride print, 12.5 x 16.9
Coll: B.N., Paris

55 (page 10)
*Kiosque à journaux, square du Bon
Marché*
Newspaper kiosk, Paris, 1912
Gold chloride print, 21.6 x 18.8
Coll: B.N., Paris

56 (page 33)
Boutique, 16 rue Dupetit-Thouars, Paris,
1912
Gold chloride print, 21.4 x 16.8
Coll: B.N., Paris

47

49

50

51

53

54

57
Eugène Atget
Boutique, 63 rue de Sèvres, Paris, 1912
Gold chloride print, 21.2 x 16.8
Coll: B.N., Paris

58 (not illustrated)
Cabaret, 25 rue des Blancs Manteaux, Paris, n.d.
Gold chloride print, 21.0 x 17.8
Coll: B.N., Paris

59 (not illustrated)
Fleuriste
Florist, 1899
Gold chloride print, 21.5 x 16.6
Coll: B.N., Paris

60 (not illustrated)
Cabaret, 54 Rue Saint André des arts, Paris, n.d.
Gold chloride print, 20.9 x 17.2
Coll: B.N., Paris

61
Au Bon Coin, rue des Haudriettes, Paris, before 1908
Gold chloride print, 21.4 x 16.8
Coll: B.N., Paris

62
Gare de Bercy, boulevard Poniatowski, Paris, 1913
Gold chloride print, 16.8 x 22.4
Coll: B.N., Paris

63
Gare de Bercy, boulevard Poniatowski, Paris, 1913
Gold chloride print, 16.8 x 21.7
Coll: B.N., Paris

64
Brassaï
Nuits parisiennes: la roue du pont élevateur, pont de Crimée
Parisian nights: the wheel of the moving bridge, pont de Crimée, Paris, about 1932
Silver print made by P. Faivre in 1987, 34.1 x 28
Coll: Madame Brassaï

65
Nuits parisiennes: 'Nestlé', XIIIème arrondissement
Parisian nights: 'Nestlé', XIIIème arrondissement, about 1935
Silver print made by P. Faivre, 1988, 33.8 x 26.2
Coll: Madame Brassaï

66
Nuits parisiennes: promenade parisienne avec L.P. Fargue
Parisian nights: a walk with L.P. Fargue, about 1935
Silver print made by P. Faivre in 1988, 34.1 x 24.8
Coll: Madame Brassaï

57

62

63

64

65

66

67

Brassaï
Nuits parisiennes: à Belleville
Parisian nights: Belleville, about 1935
Silver print made by P. Faivre in 1988,
33.8 x 27
Coll: Madame Brassaï

68

Avenue de l'Observatoire: Lèon-Paul Fargue, 1932
Silver print, 38 x 28.4
Coll: Madame Brassaï

69

La statue du Maréchal Ney dans le brouillard, avenue de l'Observatoire
Fog and the statute of Marshal Ney, about 1932
Silver print, 40.5 x 56.7
Coll: M.N.A.M., Paris

70

Colonne Morris dans le brouillard
A Morris column in the fog, about 1932
Silver print, 39 x 29.4
Coll: M.N.A.M., Paris

71

Le café des Deux Magots, 1943
Silver print, 30.4 x 23.7
Coll: Madame Brassaï

72 (page 35)
Couple d'amoureux dans un café
Lovers in a café, 1932
Silver print, 39.5 x 29.6
Coll: M.N.A.M., Paris

67

69

70

68

71

73
Brassaï
Paris de nuit: les amoureux
Paris by night: the lovers, 1932
Silver print, 34.3 x 25.9
Coll: Madame Brassaï

74
Le pont Neuf dans la brume
Pont Neuf in the fog, 1937
Silver print, 39.7 x 29.9
Coll: Madame Brassaï

75
Nuits de Longchamp, 1937
Silver print, 39.9 x 29.9
Coll: Madame Brassaï

76
*Paris de nuit: vue nocturne de
Notre-Dame sur Paris et la Tour
Saint-Jacques*
Paris by night: view from Notre Dame
over Paris and the Tour St Jacques,
1933
Silver print, 40.5 x 30.3
Coll: Madame Brassaï

77 (page 34)
*Paris de nuit: péripaticienne vue de dos,
quartier d'Italie*
Paris by night: street-walker from the
back, 1932,
Silver print, 39.9 x 29.5
Coll: Madame Brassaï

78 (page 36)
Paris de nuit: Chez Suzy
Paris by night: Chez Suzy, about 1932
Silver print, 29.8 x 22.5
Coll: Madame Brassaï

76

73

75

74

79
Brassaï
Les deux amies
The girlfriends, 1932
Silver print, 35.9 x 27.3
Coll: Madame Brassaï

80
Armoire à glace dans une maison de passe
Wardrobe mirror in a brothel, about 1932
Silver print, 39.8 x 30.1
Coll: M.N.A.M., Paris

81
Paris de nuit: Chez Suzy, rue Grégoire de Tours
Paris by night: Chez Suzy, about 1932
Silver print, 21.8 x 28.7
Coll: Madame Brassaï

82 (page 37)
Paris de nuit: un complet pour deux, bal Magic City
Paris by night: young couple sharing the same suit, about 1931
Silver print, 30 x 23.8
Coll: Madame Brassaï

83
La présentation, chez Suzy, rue Grégoire de Tours
Introductions, chez Suzy, rue Grégoire de Tours, about 1932
Silver print, 39.2 x 29.2
Coll: M.N.A.M., Paris

84
Bijou au Bar de la lune, Montmartre
Bijou in the Bar de la lune, about 1932
Silver print, 39.6 x 28.2
Coll: M.N.A.M., Paris

85
Quai de Bercy, about 1932
Silver print, 40.4 x 29.8
Coll: Madame Brassaï

79

80

81

85

83

84

140

86
Brassaï
Le mur de la Santé
The wall of the Santé prison, 1932
Silver print, 32.7 x 23.5
Coll: Madame Brassaï

87
L'atelier de Picasso: 2 têtes de mort en papier
Picasso's studio: 2 paper skulls, 1946
Silver print made by P. Faivre in 1987, 23.7 x 30.3
Coll: Madame Brassaï

88
L'atelier de Picasso: visage-masque en papier
Picasso's studio: paper face-mask, 1946
Silver print made by P. Faivre in 1987, 23.7 x 30.3
Coll: Madame Brassaï

89
L'atelier de Picasso: moulage de papier froissé
Picasso's studio: model in crumpled paper, 1944
Silver print made by P. Faivre in 1987, 23.7 x 30.3
Coll: Madame Brassaï

90
L'atelier de Picasso: morceau de plâtre cannelé
Picasso's studio: fragment of fluted plaster, 1944
Silver print made by P. Faivre in 1987, 23.7 x 30.3
Coll: Madame Brassaï

© Madame G. Brassaï

86

90

88

89

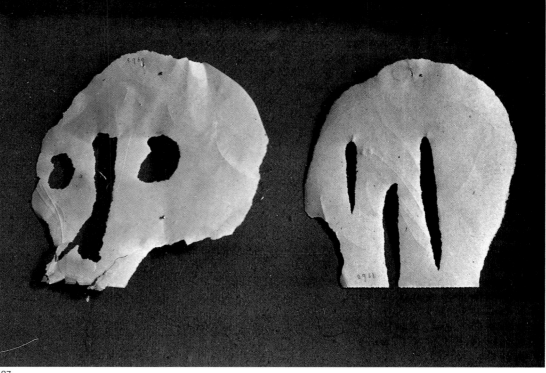
87

91 (page 38)
Jacques-Henri Lartigue
Au Carlton, Vichy, août 1922
At the Carlton, Vichy, August 1922
Silver print made by Yvon le Marlec,
1987, 50.5 x 27
Coll: Donation J.H. Lartigue

92
Bibi, 1923
Silver print made by Yvon le Marlec,
1987, 50.5 x 27
Coll: Donation J.H. Lartigue

93
Biarritz, 1930
Silver print made by Yvon le Marlec,
1987, 50.5 x 27
Coll: Donation J.H. Lartigue

94
Mamie, Bibi and Catherine, Berck, 1924
Silver print made by Yvon le Marlec,
1987
27 x 50.5
Coll: Donation J.H. Lartigue

95 (page 41)
*Gerard Willemetz and Dani, Royan, July
1926*
Silver print made by Yvon le
Marlec,1987, 50.5 x 27
Coll: Donation J.H. Lartigue

96 (page 39)
*Chouchou, tournage de Feu' de
Baroncelli, Epinay, décembre 1926*
Chouchou shooting Fire' by Baroncelli,
Epinay, December 1926
Silver print made by Yon le Marlec,1987,
50.5 x 27
Coll: Donation J.H. Lartigue

97 (page 38)
Bibi, London, October 1926
Silver print made by Yvon le Marlec,
1987, 27 x 50.5
Coll: Donation J.H. Lartigue

92

93

94

98
Jacques-Henri Lartigue
Autoportrait, les dunes de Merlimont
Self-portrait on the Merlimont dunes,
1924
Silver print made by Yvon le Marlec,
1987, 27 x 50.5
Coll: Donation J.H. Lartigue

99
*Inauguration de l'autodrome de
Montlhery,*
Opening of the Montlhery race-track,
1924
Silver print made by Yvon le Marlec,
1987, 27 x 50.5
Coll: Donation J.H. Lartigue

100
*Anniversaire de Dani, Royan, 23 août
1926*
Dani's birthday, Royan, 23 August 1926
Silver print made by Yvon le Marlec,
1987, 27 x 50.5
Coll: Donation J.H. Lartigue

101
*Sala au Rocher de la Vierge, Biarritz,
août 1927*
Sala at the Rock of the Virgin, Biarritz,
August 1927
Silver print made by Yvon le Marlec,
1987, 27 x 50.5
Coll: Donation J.H. Lartigue

102 (page 41)
*Bibi, l'ombre et le reflet, Hendaye, août
1927*
Bibi, shadow and reflection, Hendaye,
August 1927
Silver print made by Yvon le Marlec,
1987, 50.5 x 27
Coll: Donation J.H. Lartigue

98

99

100

101

103

Jacques-Henri Lartigue

Bibi, installation du nouvel appartement par Djo Bourgeois, Neuilly, juillet 1927
Bibi, in the new apartment by Djo Bourgeois, Neuilly, July 1927
Silver print made by Yvon le Marlec, 1987, 27 x 50.5
Coll: Donation J.H. Lartigue

104

Premier et dernier vol de la 'Chauve-souris'
The first and last flight of the 'Bat'
The first meeting of airplanes without engines. Combegrasse, August 1922
Silver print made by Yvon le Marlec, 1987, 27 x 50.5
Coll: Donation J.H. Lartigue

105

Luigi, chanteur des rues, frontière italienne, septembre 1927
Luigi, street singer, at the Italian frontier, September 1927
Silver print made by Yvon le Marlec, 1987, 27 x 50.5
Coll: Donation J.H. Lartigue

106 (page 40)

Mamie, Bibi et Jean le chauffeur: automobile Hispano-Suiza 32 HP sur la route d'Houlgate, avril 1927
Mamie, Bibi and Jean the chauffeur: Hispano-Suiza 32 HP car on the road to Houlgate, April 1927
Silver print made by Yvon le Marlec, 1987, 27 x 50.5
Coll: Donation J.H. Lartigue

107 (not illustrated)

Passage du Tour de France, col des Aravis, juillet 1928
The Tour de France at the Col des Aravis, July 1928
Silver print made by Yvon le Marlec, 1987, 27 x 50.5
Coll: Donation J.H. Lartigue

104

105

108

The Grand Prix d'Antibes, May 1929
Silver print made by Yvon le Marlec,
1987, 27 x 50.5
Coll: Donation J.H. Lartigue

109

Déménagement, rue Leroux, Paris,
Juillet 1927
Moving house, Paris, July 1927
Silver print made by Yvon le Marlec,
1987, 27 x 50.5
Coll: Donation J.H. Lartigue

110
André Kertèsz
Circus, May 1919
Silver print, 25 x 20
Coll: M.N.A.M., Paris

111
Square la nuit
A square at night, Paris 1926
Silver print, 25 x 20
Coll: M.N.A.M., Paris

108

109

110

111

112
André Kertèsz
Assiette cassée
Broken plate, 1929
Silver print, 20 x 25
Coll: M.N.A.M., Paris

113
*L'été: un soir d'orage de ma fenêtre, rue
de Vanves*
A summer evening's storm seen from
my window in the rue de Vanves, 1925
Silver print, 20 x 25
Coll: M.N.A.M., Paris

114
Eiffel Tower, 1929
Silver print, 20 x 25
Coll: M.N.A.M., Paris

115 (page 47)
Trottoir
Pavement, 1929
Silver print, 25 x 20
Coll: M.N.A.M., Paris

116
Les lunettes et la pipe de Mondrian
Mondrian's glasses and pipe, 1926
Silver print, 20 x 25
Coll: M.N.A.M., Paris

117
Chez Mondrian, Paris
At Mondrian's house, Paris, 1926
Silver print, 25 x 20
Coll: M.N.A.M., Paris

118
Bistrot, 1927
Silver print, 25 x 20
Coll: M.N.A.M., Paris

119 (page 44)
Danseur burlesque
Burlesque dancer, 1926
Silver print, 25 x 20
Coll: M.N.A.M., Paris

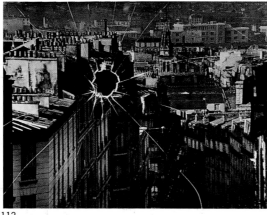

112

113

114

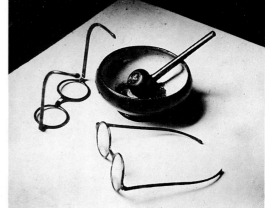

116

117

118

120
André Kertèsz
Autoportrait
Self-portrait, 1927
Silver print, 25 x 20
Coll: M.N.A.M., Paris

121 (page 43)
Une fenêtre, quai Voltaire
A window in the quai Voltaire, Paris,
1928
Silver print, 25 x 20
Coll: M.N.A.M., Paris

122
Meudon, 1928
Silver print, 25 x 20
Coll: M.N.A.M., Paris

123 (not illustrated)
Nageur sous l'eau
Underwater swimmer, 1917
Silver print, 20 x 25
Coll: M.N.A.M., Paris

124
Place Gambetta, 1928
Silver print, 25 x 20
Coll: M.N.A.M., Paris

125
Aux Halles
In Les Halles, 1928
Silver print, 20 x 25
Coll: M.N.A.M., Paris

126
Fourchette
Fork, 1928
Silver print, 20 x 25
Coll: M.N.A.M., Paris

127
Carrefour, Blois
Crossroads, Blois, 1930
Silver print, 20 x 25
Coll: M.N.A.M., Paris

120

122

124

125

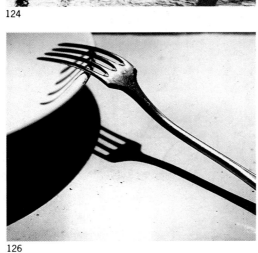
126

127

147

128
André Kertèsz
Fête foraine
Fun-fair, 1931
Silver print, 25 x 20
Coll: M.N.A.M., Paris

129
Elisabeth, 1931
Silver print, 25 x 20
Coll: M.N.A.M., Paris

130
Le Louvre à travers la vitre de l'horloge de l'Institut
The Louvre from window of the clock in the Institut, 1932
Silver print, 25 x 20
Coll: M.N.A.M., Paris

131
Bobino, 1932
Silver print, 21.8 x 19.7
Coll: M.N.A.M., Paris

132
Paris, 1933
Silver print, 24.7 x 19.2
Coll: M.N.A.M., Paris

128

130

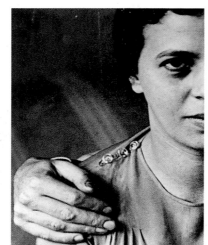
129

131

132

133
André Kertèsz
Distortion no. 6, 1933
Silver print, 25 x 20
Coll: M.N.A.M., Paris

134 (page 45)
Distortion no. 40, 1933
Silver print, 20 x 25
Coll: M.N.A.M., Paris

135 (page 42)
Dubo, Dubon, Dubonnet, 1934
Silver print, 25 x 20
Coll: M.N.A.M., Paris

136
Tulipe mélancolique
Melancholy tulip, 1939
Silver print, 25 x 20
Coll: M.N.A.M., Paris

137
Christopher Street, 1950
Silver print, 25 x 20
Coll: M.N.A.M., Paris

138
Le square du Vert Galant, 1963
Silver print, 25 x 20
Coll: M.N.A.M., Paris

139 (not illustrated)
IIIrd Avenue, New York, 1937
Silver print, 25 x 20
Coll: M.N.A.M., Paris

140 (not illustrated)
Puddle, 1967
Silver print, 25 x 20
Coll: M.N.A.M., Paris

141 (page 46)
Martinique, 1972
Silver print, 20 x 25
Coll: M.N.A.M., Paris

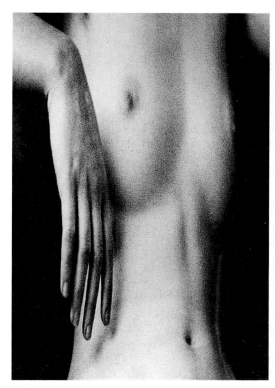
133

136

137

138

149

DADA AND SURREALISM

142
Roger Parry
Thread and starfish, 1932
Photogram and silver print, 15 x 10.3
Coll: M.N.A.M., Paris

143
Untitled, about 1930
Photogram and silver print, 24.7 x 22.4
Coll: M.N.A.M, Paris

144 (page 53)
Untitled, about 1928-1930
Photomontage, silver print, 17.9 x 14.3
Coll: M.N.A.M., Paris

145
Florence Henri
Sans titre (autoportrait)
Untitled (selfportrait), 1932
Silver print, 10 x 7.8
Coll: M.N.A.M., Paris

146 (page 54)
L'assiette et le miroir
Saucer and mirror, 1931
Silver print, 24.5 x 18.7
Coll: B.N., Paris

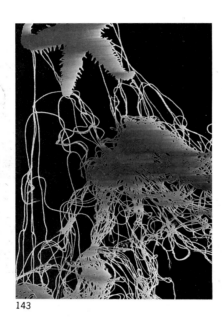

143

142

145

147
Florence Henri
Feuilles
Leaves, n.d.
Silver print, 29.6 x 20 8
Coll: B.N., Paris

148
Les fenêtres
Windows, 1930
Silver print, 29 x 20.7
Coll: B.N., Paris

149
Robert Bresson
Untitled, about 1932
Silver print, 27.6 x 21.3
Coll: M.N.A.M., Paris

150 (page 55)
Lunar landscape, 1932
Silver print, 16 x 11.9
Coll: M.N.A.M., Paris

151
Hans Bellmer
La poupée
The doll, 1935
Silver print, 47.5 x 70
Coll: André François Petit

152 (not illustrated)
Die Puppe
The doll, 1936-49
Silver print coloured with aniline,
41 x 32.9
Coll: M.N.A.M., Paris

153 (page 52)
La poupée
The doll, 1949
Silver print coloured with aniline,
100 x 101
Coll: M.N.A.M., Paris

154
La poupée
The doll, 1949
Silver print coloured with aniline,
101 x 101
Coll: M.N.A.M., Paris

155 (not illustrated)
La poupée
The doll, 1949
Eleven prints made for the GLM edition
of *La Poupée* (Paris 1949). Silver print
coloured with aniline
Coll: Bihl-Bellmer

147

149

148

154

156 (page 57)
Brassaï
Graffiti, 1934
Silver print, 24 x18
Coll: M.N.A.M., Paris

157
Graffiti: l'amour
Graffiti: love, 1934
Silver print, 29.5 x 23.5
Coll: M.N.A.M., Paris

158 (page 56)
Graffiti: la mort
Graffiti: death, 1934
Silver print, 48.8 x 38.7
Coll: M.N.A.M., Paris

159
Graffiti: la magie
Graffiti: magic, 1934
Silver print, 84 x 54
Coll: M.N.A.M., Paris

160
Graffiti: la magie, démon de Belleville
Graffiti: magic, the Belleville demon,
1955
Silver print, 141 x 106.3
Coll: M.N.A.M., Paris

161 (page 60)
Jean Painlevé
Bust of a sea-horse, about 1930
Silver print, 60.5 x 49.5
Coll: M.N.A.M., Paris

162
Jacques-André Boiffard
Renée Jacobi, 1930/33
Silver print, 28.3 x 18.8
Coll: M.N.A.M., Paris

163
Untitled, about 1932/33
Silver print, 16.1 x 20
Coll: M.N.A.M., Paris

164 (page 61)
Photogramme, about 1932/33
Silver print, 29.9 x 23.9
Coll: M.N.A.M., Paris

165
Les rayons brisés
Broken rays, about 1932/33
Silver print made by P. Gassman in
1985, 22.5 x 18.4
Coll: M.N.A.M., Paris

166
Raoul Hausmann
Nos Dames de Paris, 1939
Silver print made by R. Vuillez, 1977,
34.7 x 26.7
Coll: M.N.A.M. Paris

157

159

160

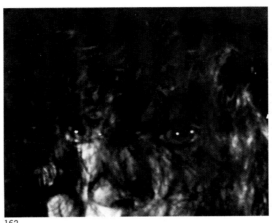
162

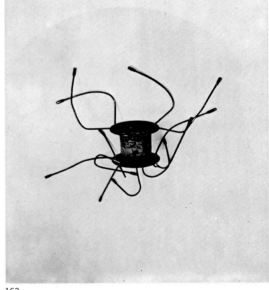
163

166

167 (page 58)
Raoul Hausmann
La balançoire
The swing, 1948
Photocollage, 27.2 x 25.1
Coll: M.N.A.M., Paris

168
Untitled, 1932
Photocollage, 32.4 x 27.9
Coll: M.N.A.M., Paris

169
Corbeilles de lumière
Baskets of light, n.d.
Three silver prints made by R. Vuillez,
1977, 29.7 x 21.5 each
Coll: M.N.A.M., Paris

170 (page 59)
Erwin Blumenfeld
L'âme du torse
The soul of the torso, 1934
Photomontage and silver print, 29 x 22
Coll: M.N.A.M., Paris

171
M's torso in mirror, 1937/38
Silver print, 34.7 x 27.4
Coll: M.N.A.M., Paris

172
Man Ray
Man, 1919 (integration of shadows)
Silver print, 24 x 18
Coll: M.N.A.M., Paris

173
La femme
Woman, 1920
Silver print, 38.8 x 29.1
Coll: M.N.A.M., Paris

174 (page 62)
Objects, 1926
Silver print, 29 x 22.5
Coll: B.N., Paris

169

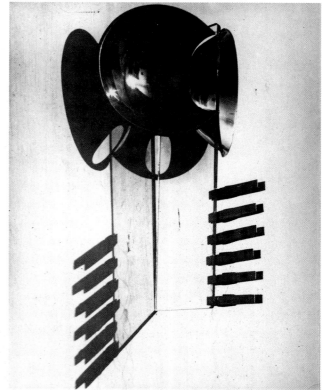

172

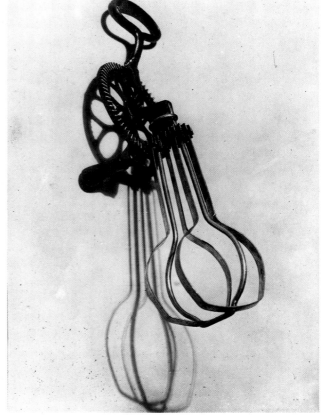

173

175
Man Ray
Le suicide
The suicide, 1926
Silver print, 22.8 x 16.8
Coll: M.N.A.M., Paris

176 (page 48)
Tête (d'après un autochrome)
Head, after an autochrome, 1929
Silver print, 29.3 x 22.7
Coll: B.N., Paris

177 (not illustrated)
Femmes
Women, 1929
Silver print, 29.6 x 22.9
Coll: B.N, Paris

178
Venus, 1929
Silver print, 29, 2 x 22
Coll: B.N., Paris

179
Lee Miller, 1930
Silver print, 22.6 x 17.4
Coll: M.N.A.M., Paris

180 (page 64)
La Marquise Casati, 1930
Silver print,
14.8 x 10
M.N.A.M., Paris
Inventaire 1987-898

181 (page 65)
Femme endormie
Sleeping woman, 1931
Solarised silver print, 21.2 x 29.1
Coll: B.N., Paris

182
Meret Oppenheim, 1933
Silver print
23.8 x 17.1
Coll: M.N.A.M., Paris

175

179

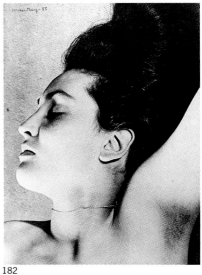

182

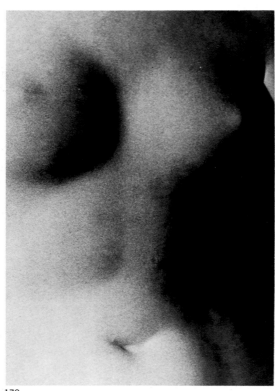

178

183

183
Man Ray
Fireworks, 1934
Silver print
29, 2 x 22, 5
Coll: M.N.A.M., Paris

184 (page 67)
A l'heure de l'Observatoire, les amoureux
At the hour of the Observatory, the lovers, 1932
Two silver prints mounted, 17.1 x 21,8
Coll: M.N.A.M., Paris

185
Sans titre (nu avec reflecteur)
Untitled (nude with lamp), about 1930
Silver print, 29.4 x 22.3
Coll: B.N, Paris

186
Objet mathématique
Mathematical object, 1936
Silver print, 29, 7 x 23, 1
Coll: M.N.A.M., Paris

187 (not illustrated)
229 Boulevard Raspail
Silver print, 1928
Coll: Lucien Treillard

188
Sans titre (feuille morte)
Untitled (dead leaf)
Silver print, 23.8 x 19.8
Coll: M.N.A.M., Paris

189 (page 63)
Autoportrait
Self portrait, 1932
Silver print, 26.4 x 21.6
Coll: B.N., Paris

190
La bouche
The mouth, 1930
Silver print, 17.4 x 22,3
Coll: B.N, Paris

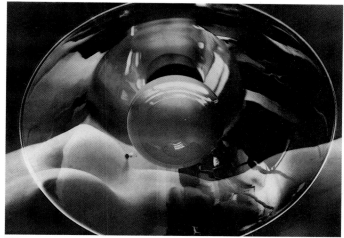

185

186

188

190

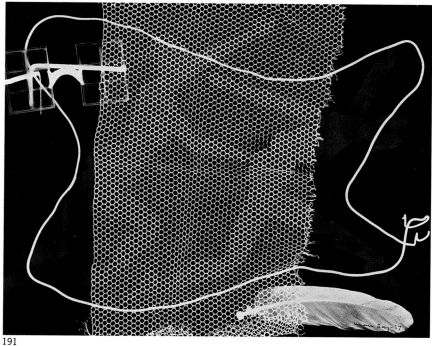

191

155

191
Man Ray
La poursuite
The pursuit, 1937
Rayograph silver print, 29, 8 x 39, 2
Coll: M.N.A.M., Paris

192
Rayograph,
Silver print, 29.8 x 23.8
Coll: B.N., Paris

193
Place de la Concorde, about 1926
Silver print, 29.5 x 22.9
Coll: B.N., Paris

194
Rayograph, 1927
Silver print, 25 x 30
Coll: B.N., Paris

195
Rayograph, 1922
Silver print, 23.8 x 17.8
Coll: B.N., Paris

196
Terrain vague
Unknown land, about 1926
Silver print, 29.2 x 21.7
Coll: B.N., Paris

197
Arums
Lillies, 1930
Solarised silver print, 28.5 x 22.9
Coll: B.N., Paris

198 (page 66)
Noire et blanche
Black and white, 1926
Silver print, 23 x 17.5
Coll: M.N.A.M., Paris

199 (not illustrated)
La lune se leve sur l'île de Niäs
The moon rises on the isle of Nias, 1926
Silver print, 14 x 9
Coll: M.N.A.M., Paris

200 (page 68)
Maurice Tabard
Tête au chapeau, oeil double
Head with hat and double eye, 1929
Surimpression silver print, 23 x 17
Coll: M.N.A.M, Paris

194

196

197

192

201 (page 69)
Maurice Tabard
Untitled, 1929
Silver print, 24 x 17.9
Coll: M.N.A.M., Paris

202
Untitled, 1930
Silver print, made by Pierre Gassmann in
1981, 30 x 22.9
Coll: M.N.A.M., Paris

203
Le gant et la bouteille sous les toits
The glove and the bottle under the
eaves, 1929
Silver print, 23.5 x 17.3
Coll: B.N., Paris

204
Deux guitares
Two guitars, 1932
Silver print, 39.4 x 29.1
Coll: B.N., Paris

205
Juan les Pins, 1935
Solarised silver print, 39,7x28,8
Coll. B. N., Paris

206 (not illustrated)
Raoul Ubac
Visage dans un miroir
Face in a mirror, 1937
Silver print, 29.3 x 27.8
Coll: B.N., Paris

207 (page 70)
Le combat de Penthésilée 14
The combat of Penthesilea 14, 1937
Silver print, 38.4 x 27.5
Coll: B.N., Paris

208 (not illustrated)
L'atelier
The studio, 1936
Photomontage, silver print, 53 x 62.5
Coll: Galerie Octant

209
Rue derrière la gare
Street behind the station, 1936
Photomontage, silver print, 59.5 x 79.7
Coll: Galerie Octant

210
Corps ensablés
Bodies in sand
Negative photomontage, silver print,
29.8 x 39.7
Coll: M.N.A.M., Paris

211 (page 71)
La nebuleuse
Nebula, 1939
Burnt silver print, 40 x 28
Coll: M.N.A.M., Paris

200

203

204

205

209

RAPPORTAGE II

212 (not illustrated)
Henri Cartier-Bresson
Chauffeurs de taxi, Berlin
Berlin taxi-drivers, 1931
Silver print, 24 x 36
Coll: B.N., Paris

213
Hyéres (France), 1932
Silver print, 24 x 36
Coll: B.N., Paris

214
Enterrement d'un acteur comique,
Burial of an actor, Paris 1932
Silver print, 24 x 36
Coll: B.N., Paris

215 (not illustrated)
Alicante (Spain), 1933
Silver print, 24 x 36
Coll: B.N., Paris

216 (not illustrated)
Granada (Spain), 1933
Silver print, 24 x 36
Coll: B.N., Paris

217
Granada (Spain), 1933
Silver print, 24 x 36
Coll: B.N., Paris

213

214

217

218
Henri Cartier-Bresson
Valencia (Spain), 1933
Silver print, 24 x 36
Coll: B.N., Paris

219
Madrid, 1933
Silver print, 24 x 36
Coll: B.N., Paris

220
Seville , 1933
Silver print, 24 x 36
Coll: B.N., Paris

221 (page 77)
Trieste (Italy), 1933
Silver print, 24 x 36
Coll: B.N., Paris

222
Salerno (Italy), 1933
Silver print, 24 x 36
Coll: B.N., Paris

223
Mexico, 1934
Silver print, 36 x 24
Coll: B.N., Paris

218

219

220

222

223

224
Henri Cartier-Bresson
Prostituées à Mexico
Mexican prostitutes, 1934
Silver print, 24 x 36
Coll: B.N., Paris

225 (page 76)
Au bord de la Marne
On the banks of the Marne, France,
1938
Silver print, 24 x 36
Coll: B.N., Paris

226
*Exercices de gymnastique pour occuper
les refugiés du camp Kurukshetra*
Gymnastic exercise for the occupants of
the Kurukshetra refugee camp, Punjab,
1947
Silver print, 24 x 36
Coll: B.N., Paris

227
Femmes musulmanes en prière
Moslem women at prayer, Srinagar,
1947
Silver print, 24 x 36
Coll: B.N., Paris

228
Rizières à Sumatra
Sumatran rice-growers, 1949
Silver print, 24 x 36
Coll: B.N., Paris

229
Danseurs en transes
Possessed dancers, Bali, 1949
Silver print, 24 x 26
Coll: B.N., Paris

224

226

227

228

229

230

Henri Cartier-Bresson

Queue devant une banque avant l'arrivée des communistes

Queue in front of a bank before the arrival of the Communists, Shanghai, 1949

Silver print, 24 x 36

Coll: B.N., Paris

231

Aquila des Abruzzes (Italy), 1952

Silver print, 24 x 36

Coll: B.N., Paris

232

Torcello (Italy), 1954

Silver print, 24 x 36

Coll: B.N., Paris

233

Syphnos (Greece), 1961

Silver print, 24 x 36

Coll: B.N., Paris

230

231

232

233

234
Henri Cartier-Bresson
Greece, 1961
Silver print, 24 x 36
Coll: B.N., Paris

235
Sardinia, 1963
Silver print, 24 x 36
Coll: B.N., Paris

30
236
Mexico, 1964
Silver print, 24 x 36
Coll: B.N., Paris

237
Prirem (Yugoslavia), 1965
Silver print, 24 x 36
Coll: B.N., Paris

238 (not illustrated)
*Funérailles d'un acteur du théâtre
kabuki*
Funeral of a *kabuki* actor, Tokyo, 1966
Silver print, 24 x 36
Coll: B.N., Paris

239
Lavandiéres
Washerwomen, Ahmedabad, 1967
Silver print, 24 x 36
Coll: B.N., Paris

234

235

236

237

239

240
Henri Cartier-Bresson
Turkey, 1965
Silver print, 24 x 36
Coll: B.N., Paris

241 (not illustrated)
Ahmedabad, (India), 1967
Silver print, 24 x 36
Coll: B.N., Paris

242
Simiane la Rotonde (France), 1969
Silver print, 24 x 36
Coll: B.N., Paris

243
Robert Doisneau
Vers la Poterne des Peupliers
Near the Poterne des Peupliers, Paris,
1934
Silver print
Artist's collection

244
Quai du port, rue Denfert-Rochereau
Quayside, rue Denfert-Rochereau, St
Denis, 1945
Silver print
Artist's collection

245
Les fréres, rue du docteur Lecéne
The brothers, rue du docteur Lecéne,
Paris, 1934
Silver print, 31 x 24
Coll: M.N.A.M., Paris , on loan from
F.N.A.C

240

242

243

244

245

246
Robert Doisneau
*La stricte intimité, rue Marcellin
Berthold*
A private wedding, rue Marcelin
Berthold, Montrouge, 1945
Silver print
Artist's collection

247
La concierge, rue Jacob
The concierge, rue Jacob, Paris, 1945
Silver print
Artist's collection

248 (page 80)
Les baigneurs de La Varenne
Bathers at La Varenne, 1945
Silver print
Artist's collection

249 (page 82)
Café noir et blanc,
The black and white café,
avenue du Général Galliéni, Joinville le
Pont, 1948
Silver print
Artist's collection

250 (page 81)
*Un regard oblique, tableau de Wagner
dans la vitrine de la Galerie Romi, rue de
Seine*
A look sideways: painting by Wagner in
the window of the Galerie Romi, rue de
Seine, Paris, 1948
Silver print
Artist's collection

251
Valse du 14 Juillet
Waltz: Bastille Day, 1949
Silver print, 30.1 x 23.5
Coll: M.N.A.M, Paris

252 (page 75)
*Mademoiselle Anita du Dancing de 'La
boule rouge', rue de Lappe*
Mademoiselle Anita, from the dancehall
La boule rouge, rue de Lappe, Paris,
1950
Silver print, 31 x 25
Coll: M.N.A.M., Paris, on loan from
F.N.A.C.

253
Les paroissiens de Saint-Médard
The parishioners of St Médard, Paris,
1951
Silver print
Artist's collection

254 (page 72)
Coco, 1952
Silver print
Artist's collection

255
La porte de l'Enfer, Boulevard de Clichy
The gate of Hell, Boulevard de Clichy,
Paris, 1952
Silver print
Artist's collection

246

247

251

253

255

256

256
Robert Doisneau
*Le baiser, place de l'Hôtel de Ville, Paris,
1950*
The kiss, place de l'Hôtel de Ville, Paris,
1950
Silver print
Artist's collection

257
*Les touristes du Paris by night au 'Petit
Balcon', passage Thière*
Tourists doing „Paris by Night" at the
'Petit Balcon', passage Thière, Paris,
1953
Silver print, 23 x 34
Coll: M.N.A.M., Paris, , on loan from
F.N.A.C.

257

258

258
Boulevard de la Chapelle, Paris, 1953
Silver print
Artist's collection

259
Le manége de Monsieur Barré
Monsieur Barré's roundabout, 1955
Silver print
Artist's collection

260 (page 83)
Les gosses de la place Hèbert
Kids from the place Hèbert, Paris 1957
Silver print
Artist's collection

259

261 (page 78)
William Klein
*Quatre têtes au coin de Broadway et de
la 33ème rue*
Four heads, corner of Broadway and
33rd St., 1954
Silver print made by Remy
Petit-Demange, 1986, 43.3 x 32.3
Coll: M.N.A.M., Paris

262
Gun 1, 103rd St., New York, 1954
Silver print made by Rémy
Petit-Demange, 1986, 45.3 x 33.3
Coll: M.N.A.M., Paris

263 (page 79)
Coney Island l'hiver
Coney Island in winter, New York, 1955
Silver print made by Rémy
Petit-Demange, 1986, 32.4 x 44.9
Coll: M.N.A.M., Paris

264
Gardien de nuit
Night watchman, New York, 1955
Silver print made by Rémy
Petit-Demange, 1986, 44.9 x 36.2
Coll: M.N.A.M., Paris

264

262

265 (page 79)
Terrasse de café
Café terrace, Paris, 1980
Silver print made by Remy
Petit-Demange, 1986, 27.5 x 45.8
Coll: M.N.A.M., Paris

266
Izis
Place Falguière, Paris, 1947
Silver print, 26.8 x 21.8
Artist's collection

267
Chevaux aux yeux bleus et mal peints
Horses with blue eyes, badly painted,
from *Le grand bal du printemps,* 1951
Silver print, 33 x 27
Coll: B.N., Paris

268
Le premier Mai, place d'Alésia
The first of May, at the place d'Alésia,
from *Le grand bal du printemps,* 1951
Silver print, 28.3 x 33.5
Coll: B.N., Paris

269 (page 86)
*Lagny, parade pour une femme
crocodile*
The crocodile lady sideshow, Lagny,
1959, from *Le cirque d'Izis,* 1965
Silver print, 35.5 x 24
Coll: B.N., Paris

270 (page 84)
Cracheur de feu
Fire-eater, boulevard Rochechouart,
1959, from *Le cirque d'Izis,* 1965
Silver print, 24 x 33.5
Coll: B.N., Paris

271 (not illustrated)
Paris, quai de l'Arsenal, péniche
Barge, quai de l'Arsenal, Paris, 1965,
from *Paris des poètes,* 1977
Silver print, 33 x 26.7
Coll: B.N., Paris

272
Jeune Colosse
Young Colossus, n.d.
Silver print
Artist's collection

273 (page 85)
Boulevard de Clichy, n.d.
Silver print, 22, 8 x 21, 8
Artist's collection

274
Edouard Boubat
La petite fille aux feuilles mortes
Little girl in dead leaves, Luxembourg
gardens, Paris, 1946
Silver print, 29.5 x 21
Coll: B.N., Paris

275
Femme couronnée de fleurs
Woman crowned with flowers, Portugal,
1958
Silver print, 33 x 29
Coll: B.N., Paris

268

267

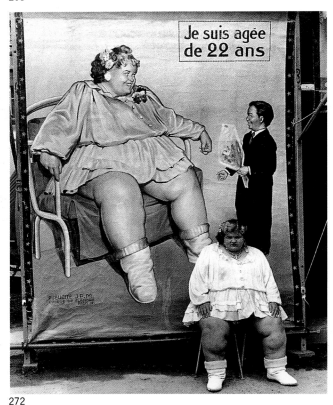

272

274

275

276
Edouard Boubat
Poule sous un arbre
Chicken and tree, near Pan, 1950
Silver print, 29 x 37
Coll: B.N., Paris

277 (page 87)
Petits garçons jouant à la guerre
Parisian children playing at soldiers,
1954
Silver print, 23.5 x 35.8
Coll: B.N., Paris

278 (page 88)
*Enfants jouant dans la neige au jardin du
Luxembourg*
Children playing in the snow,
Luxembourg gardens, Paris, 1955
Silver print, 25.5 x 39.5
Coll: B.N., Paris

279
Femme couronnée d'algues
Woman with crown of seaweed,
Portugal, 1958
Silver print, 39.5 x 30
Coll: B.N., Paris

280 (not illustrated)
Fête de la Vierge, près de Porto
Feast of the Virgin, near Opporto, 1958
Silver print, 27 x 39.5
Coll: B.N., Paris

281
*Enfant costumé en ange, fête de la
Vierge, près de Porto*
Child dressed as an angel, Feast of the
Virgin, near Opporto, Portugal, 1958
Silver print, 39, 5 x 27
Coll: B.N., Paris

282 (page 99)
Lucette enceinte de Clémence
Lucette carrying Clémence, Paris, 1971
Silver print, 40 x 24.5
Coll: B.N., Paris

283
*Maçons sur un chantier aux Champs
Elysées*
Stone-masons at work in the Champs
Elysées, Paris, 1957
Silver print, 28 x 39,5
Coll: B.N., Paris

284
Marins dans les vergues
Sailors in the yards, Italy, 1957
Silver print, 26, 5 x 39
Coll: B.N., Paris

285
*Jeunes gens jouant du piston dans les
greniers de la Sorbonne, Paris, mai 1968*
Horn players in the attic of the
Sorbonne, Paris, May 1968
Silver print, 30 x 39.5
Coll: B.N., Paris

277

279

281

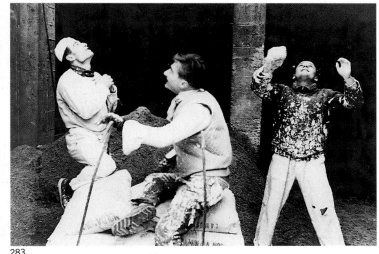

283

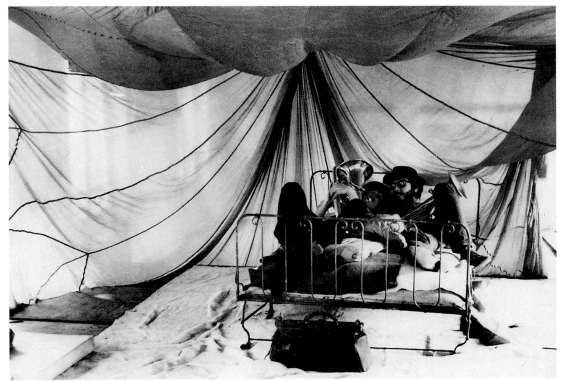

285

286
Edouard Boubat
Cirque des Muchachos, Paris, 1970
Silver print, 34 x 23.5
Coll: B.N., Paris

287
Torse de femme noire
Black woman's torso, n.d.
Silver print, 39.5 x 25
Coll: B.N., Paris

288 (page 89)
A la maniére du Douanier Rousseau
After the Douanier Rousseau, Paris,
1980
Silver print, 24 x 36
Coll: B.N., Paris

289
Trouée à travers le feuillage
A gap in the leaves, Paris, 1980
Silver print, 36 x 24
Coll: B.N., Paris

290
La lecture au parc du Luxembourg
Reading in the Luxembourg gardens,
Paris, 1980
Silver print, 24 x 26
Coll: B.N., Paris

291
Jeunes filles costumées en ange
Girls dressed as angels, Feast of the
Virgin, near Opporto, Portugal, 1958
Silver print, 27 x 39.5
Coll: B.N., Paris

286

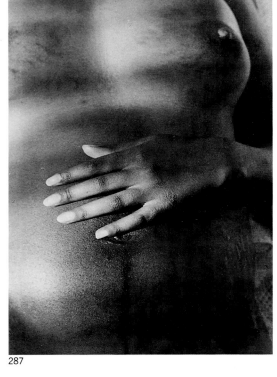
287

289

290

291

292 (page 90)
Willy Ronis
La Ciotat, été
La Ciotat, summer 1947
Silver print
Artist's collection

293 (page 91)
Place Vendôme sous la pluie
The place Vendôme in the rain, Paris,
1947
Silver print
Artist's collection

294
Fête foraine, quartier Pasteur
Local fair in the Pasteur quarter of Paris,
1947
Silver print
Artist's collection

295
*Elisabeth-Marie, Fécamp, November,
1949*
Silver print
Artist's collection

296
L'avenue Simon Bolivar,
Belleville-Ménilmontant, late winter,
1950
Silver print
Artist's collection

297 (page 92)
Nu de dos
Nude from the back, May 1955
Silver print
Artist's collection

298
Ecluse à Anvers
Lock at Antwerp, 1957
Silver print
Artist's collection

299 (page 93)
La péniche aux enfants, sur la Seine
The children's barge, on the Seine,
January 1959
Silver print
Artist's collection

300
Emmanuel Sougez
Copeaux roulés
Wood turnings, 1932
Silver print, 36.6 x 27.4
Coll: B.N., Paris

294

295

296

298

169

301
Emmanuel Sougez
Pot de jacinthes
Pot of hyacinths, 1932
Silver print, 34.9 x 25.9
Coll: B.N., Paris

302
Sardines, 1932
Silver print, 36.3 x 27.5
Coll: B.N., Paris

303
Satin et plumes
Satin and feathers, 1933
Silver print, 37.5 x 27.5
Coll: B.N., Paris

304
Quinze verres
Fifteen glasses, 1933
Silver print, 37 x 27.7
Coll: B.N., Paris

305 (page 94)
Trois poires
Three pears, 1934
Silver print, 36.7 x 26.7
Coll: B.N., Paris

306
Eperlans
Smelts, 1934
Silver print, 36.1 x 27.1
Coll: B.N., Paris

307
Lingerie
Linen, 1935
Silver print, 35.5 x 27.2
Coll: B.N., Paris

308 (page 95)
Blancs
In white, 1947
Silver print, 39.3 x 29.4
Coll: B.N., Paris

309
Copeaux
Shavings, 1932
Silver print, 36.4 x 26.8
Coll: B.N., Paris

301

302

303

304

306

307

309

170

310 (page 97)
Jean-Pierre Sudre
Le panier aux oeufs
The egg-basket, Bouley-Morin, 1953
Silver print, 21 x 27.5
Artist's collection

311
Le pot aux oeufs
The egg-pot, 1954
Platinum print, 24 x 30
Coll: M.N.A.M., Paris

312
Verre aux coquillages, Paris
Glass with shells, Paris, 1955
Silver print, 21 x 27.5
Artist's collection

313
Le lys
The lily, Bouley-Morin, 1960
Silver print, 21 x 27.5
Artist's collection

314
Bouquet aux digitales
Bouquet of foxgloves, n.d.
Silver print, 21 x 27.5
Artist's collection

315 (not illustrated)
Jean Dieuzaide
Les artichauts de montagne
Mountain artichokes, 1977
Bromide print heightened with
selenium, 32,7 x 24.6
Artist's collection

316 (page 98)
Feuille de chardon après la pluie
Thistle leaves after rain, 1978
Silver print, partly heightened with single
sulphur, 33.3 x 24.5
Coll: M.N.A.M., Paris

317 (page 96)
Aveyron, Cascade de la Roque, 1981
Bromide print heightened with
selenium, 298 x 242
Artist's collection

318
L'arum Ecrin
The Ecrin lily, 1983
Bromide print heightened with
selenium, 34.1 x 24.5
Artist's collection

314

318

171

CONTEMPORARY PHOTOGRAPHY

319
Pierre De Fenoÿl
Jardins des Tuileries, Paris, February, 1982
Silver print, 53 x 36, 1
Coll: B.N., Paris

320 (page 107)
Alexandria, June, 1983
Silver print, 52,2 x 35, 9
Coll: B.N., Paris

321 (not illustrated)
L'Arc en ciel
Rainbow, 1984
Silver print, 35, 7 x 53, 4
Coll: B.N., Paris

322 (page 111)
Paysage mouillé
Soaking landscape, 1984
Silver print, 35, 3 x 52,6
Coll: B.N., Paris

323 (not illustrated)
L'armoire á glace
The wardrobe mirror, 1986
Silver print, 48, 5 x 33, 2
Coll: B.N., Paris

324
Tom Drahos
Papiers froissés
Crumpled papers, 1981
Silver print, 43 x 43.7
Coll: M.N.A.M., Paris

325
Papiers froissés
Crumpled papers, 1982
Silver print, 42.9 x 43.2
Coll: M.N.A.M., Paris

326 (page 115)
Papiers froissés
Crumpled papers, 1982
Silver print, 43 x 43.2
Coll: M.N.A.M., Paris

319

324

323

327 (page 114)
Papiers froissés
Crumpled papers, 1982
Silver print, 43 x 43.4
Coll: M.N.A.M., Paris

328 (not illustrated)
Sans Titre
Untitled, 1984
Two cibachrome prints, each 100 x 200
Artist's collection

329 (facing page)
Patrick Faïgenbaum
Portrait, 1979
Silver print, 32, 5 x 26, 8
Coll: B.N., Paris

330 (facing page)
Portrait, 1980
Silver print, 28, 8 x 28, 8
Coll: B.N., Paris

331 (page 100)
Portrait, 1981
Silver print, 29, 8 x 29
Coll: B.N., Paris

332
Portrait, 1981
Silver print, 28, 7 x 28, 8
Coll: B.N., Paris

333 (page 112)
Bernard Faucon
La neuvième chambre d'amour
The ninth chamber of love, n.d.
Fresson process print, 60 x 60
Artist's collection

334 (not illustrated)
La tempête de neige, quatorzième
chambre d'amour
The snowstorm, fourteenth chamber of
love, n.d.
Fresson process print, 60 x 60
Artist's collection

335 (not illustrated)
La chambre en hiver, num. 1; la glace
The chamber in winter, no. 1; the mirror,
1986
Fresson process print, 60 x 60
Artist's collection

336 (page 112)
La chambre d'or; le tabernacle
The golden chamber; the tabernacle,
1987
Fresson process print, 60 x 60
Artist's collection

337
Denis Roche
26 juillet 1984. Varallo, Italie, Albergo
del Sacro Monte, chambre 3
July 26th, 1984. Varallo, Italy. Albergo
del Sacro Monte, room 3.
Two silver prints, 20 x 30
Artist's collection

338 (page 106)
22 février 1985. Lougsor, Egypte.
Habou Hotel
February 22nd, 1985. Luxor, Egypt.
Habou Hotel
Two silver prints, 20 x 30
Artist's collection

339
3 août 1985. Moulins, 'Hommage a
Signorelli'
August 3rd, 1985. Moulins. 'Homage to
Signorelli'
Silver print, 20 x 30
Artist's collection

329

330

332

337

339

173

340
Keiichi Tahara
Fenêtre numero. 1
Window no. 1, 1974
Silver print, 38.5 x 26
Private collection

341
Fenêtre numero. 38
Window no. 38, 1976
Silver print, 38 x 26
Private collection

342 (page 110)
Fenêtre, 1978
Silver print, 39 x 26.5
Private collection

343
Fenêtre. 1978
Silver print, 26.5 x 39.5
Private collection

344
Nancy Pajic-Wilson
Le Cirque: acrobates
The Circus: acrobats, 1971-83
Heavy ink print, 17 x 12.7
Coll: M.N.A.M., Paris

345
Le Cirque: acrobates
The Circus: acrobats, 1971-83
Heavy ink print, 16.5 x 11.7
Coll: M.N.A.M., Paris

346 (facing page)
Le Cirque: acrobates
The Circus: acrobats, 1971-83
Heavy ink print, 17.2 x 12.6
Coll: M.N.A.M., Paris

347 (facing page)
Le Cirque: acrobates
The Circus: acrobats, 1971-83
Heavy ink print, 16.2 x 10
Coll: M.N.A.M., Paris

348 (page 121)
Le Cirque: acrobates
The Circus: acrobats, 1971-83
Heavy ink print, 17 x 12.7
Coll: M.N.A.M., Paris

343

341

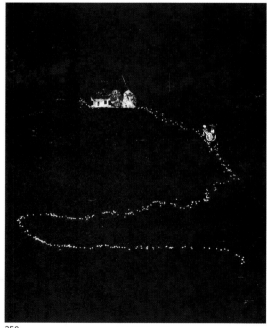

350

349 (page 108)
Christian Boltanski
Composition théâtrale
Theatrical composition, 1981
Three colour photographs, each 241 x
124.5
Coll: M.N.A.M., Paris

350
Paysage japonais
Japanese landscape, 1982
Polaroid print, 75 x 55.7
Private collection, Paris

351 (not illustrated)
Paysage japonais
Japanese landscape,1982
Polaroid print, 75 x 60
Artist's collection

352 (page 105)
Alain Fleisher
Happy days with Velasquez, 1987
Cibachrome print, 120 x 168
Coll: Galerie Michele Chomette

353 (page 109)
Patrick Bailly-Maître-Grand
Lune
Moon, 1985
Six daguerreotypes, 70x70
Coll: C.N.E.S., Toulouse

354 (page 116/7)
Pascal Kern
Fiction colorée
Fiction in colours, 1985
Two cibachrome prints, each 125 x185
Coll: M.N.A.M., Paris

355 (page 118/9)
Ernest Pignon - Ernest
Rimbaud, 1978
Charcoal drawing and photograph, 100
x 68 et 100 x 68
Coll: M.N.A.M., Paris

356 (page 120)
George Rousse
Sans titre, Sommevoire, 1946
Untitled, 1983
Cibachrome print, 192 x 240
Coll: F.N.A.C., Paris

346

347

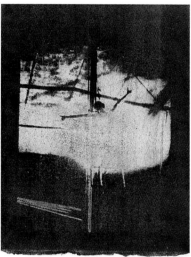
344

345

Published on behalf of Barbican Art Gallery by
Trefoil Publications Ltd.
7 Royal Parade, Dawes Road, London SW6
on the occasion of the exhibition *Art or Nature* organised by Barbican Art Gallery and the
Association Française d'Action Artistique, Ministére des Affaires Etrangéres à Paris

First Published 1988

ISBN 0 86294 130 X

Distributed exclusively in the U.S.A. and Canada by
Rizzoli International, Inc,.
597 Fifth Avenue, New York, NY 10017
ISBN 0 8478 0943 0

Designed by Langley Iddins
Edited by Joanna Toch, assisted by Charles Benn
Translated from the French by Dyanne Cullinane
Typeset by Wandsworth Typesetting Ltd.
Duotone origination by Colorlito, Milan
Printed and bound in Italy by Graphicom s.r.l.